June 19, 2019

To Eleanor,

I hope you will enjoy a Taste of

"A Slice of the Pie"

Elaine Joy Hopkins Lynch

267-207-1057 Cell

Email LAINEHOP@COMCAST.Net

D1316836

A Slice of the Pie

<u>by</u>

Elaine Py Hopkins - Lynch

With William A. Py deceased

May 14, 2018

Dear Elaine,

I hope we were helpful in adding our thoughts and corrections to your manuscript. Sometimes, as I was reading, I would forget what my task was, because I got so engrossed in your pie.

Your story is worth the telling. It has all the ingredients of life, from joy to heartache to downright, coffee through the nose, astonishing punch lines. Some were funny, and some were shocking. I soon learned not to drink beverages while proofreading your book. I am sure your family and friends will enjoy your efforts along with strangers, who happen upon it.

Great job, Love Pat, and Joe Farley

Acknowledgements

My sincere thanks to the following for their faith in me to complete this promise to my father, **William Alphonse Py.** **Carol & Andrew Farley,** who told me to keep the memories alive, **Joe & Pat Farley,** they just kept asking for more Pie. **Tammie Diehl,** a columnist for the Charlotte Sun, Pt. Charlotte, FL. who introduced me to **Create Space,** and helped with tone & mood in the story. My supportive husband, **The Great Lynch John C** who made me read the dictionary & thesaurus. **Margie Dixon Corkery, and Ruth Py** first editor, granddaughter **Brigid Hurst** in set up, **Hanna Wylesol,** for photo wrap, my **son Kevin Hopkins;** he retrieved this doc, & emailed it to me in FL, or it would be wasting away at home in PA. **Irene Kaiser, Linda Rowan,** helpful editors. **Deb & John Wilkins, and Marylin & Paul,** my Canadian friends who never gave up on me during the past six years. **Kathy Dunn** wants the first signed copy. To **my 9 siblings who let me tell a little about them.** Thanks to **my Dad in Heaven who guided me to the end.** Art by **Patrick McElroy, Henry John Hurst,** my grandson, & his mom Kathleen who helped in last edits . He is in 8th grade at Presentation BVM School, Cheltenham

Contents

Remembering our Brother Bill (11/5/45-1/11/18) and Sister Marian (3/31/54 - 9/1/17) in this prayer.✝
RICHARD M PY (12/16/53 - 1-31-19)

In 1980, I received a prayer card from Fr. Francis Mc Dermott, I keep it in my Mass Book. It reads like this:

"I give thanks to my God for all my memories of you, happy at all times in all the prayers I offer you, my living and deceased family. And this is my prayer for you:

May your love grow richer and richer yet, in fullness of its knowledge and the depth of its perception, so that you may learn to prize what is of value: may nothing cloud your progress: may you reap through Jesus Christ, the full harvest. To God's Honor and praise." St. Paul-Phil. 1:3,11

This is now my gift I share with you my readers. Love, honor, and obey your parents. Keep their memories alive and pass on all your family history. Never let it be said, "We did not know anything about our ancestors, and our past." Even though they are deceased, keep your **family alive** in your hearts and minds. ("We will always love Our parents and siblings, they will always be in our hearts".) *("To live in hearts, we leave behind, is not to die.") by… Thomas Campbell*

Just this one note: To all readers, I must have been out to lunch during **Spelling, Grammar, and Geography** while I marked time in the early years of my school days, so please excuse my errors. I am sure there are some. This is no Joke!

"A Slice of the Pie", is a true story of love, laughter, and tears, as I perceived my family and my experiences while I was growing up, in three neighborhoods in Philadelphia, PA.

All stories should end the way our lives will end. Happy and Loved, but Love can bring Life, and then Sorrow. At the end of each of our lives on earth, Our Lord will come and end all sorrow for those who **BELIEVE.**

Jesus said, "I say to you, Truly, truly whoever **believes** has eternal life." John...6 47

Dedication to My Parents.

Dad, baptized William Alphonse David Py, who, ever since I can remember, (1976) wanted to write a story, about his and our families lives. He wanted to title it, "A Slice of the Pie". Our family name is Py. Dad should have been the slice, but for a tall man he had a short life. So, I have taken his place in the story.

Dad enjoyed playing his banjo; he liked deep-sea fishing, crabbing, Pabst Blue Ribbon beer, a sweet red wine, and a pack of Camels or Lucky Strikes cigarettes. My dad stood six feet two inches tall, a very thin man, with coarse red curly hair. Most of all he loved his wife Mary, and their ten children.

Mom, baptized Mary H. Weldon used T. rather than H. She was the finest part of our Pie, (the crust) like the glue that holds it together. A very small woman, she stood no more than five feet or so tall, and weighed ninety-eight pounds, with thick blondish hair in her youth. Mother was a self-made female chef, and baker. She loved our God. mom was a devoted wife, and mother. Like dad she enjoyed a glass of red wine or a highball and her cigarettes.

Mom lovingly gave birth to the first slice of the ten of us, (me) Elaine in 1942, just over seventeen years c.1959, she shared continuing love to the last portion of the pie, a baby girl, Regina. Mom and dad raised ten little pies. Thinking back, I wonder if it should have been, "Ten Little Indians"?

We did not have many worldly things, but thanks to our mom and dad there was a lot of LOVE on Second Street, in that small six room home, with just three bedrooms and only **one** bathroom. Our home was located in the Feltonville section of Philadelphia, PA. Dad called it "Py's Wharf." Oh! only if the walls in our house had ears and could talk. I will try to tell some of dad's and our story. It will be mine since he never had the opportunity to pen it to paper. I am honoring his wish to tell about his family, and my life as a Py. Mom and dad the two of you are now in a **mansion, God's Mansion**.

A word of comfort for all

Jesus said to his disciples;

"Do not let your hearts be troubled. You have faith in God; have faith in me. In my Father's house there are many **mansions.** If there were not, would I have told you that I am going to prepare a place for you? And if I go and prepare a place for you, I will come back again and take you to myself, so that where I am, you also may be. Where I am going, you know the way." Thomas said to him, "Master, we do not know where you are going; how can we know the way." Jesus said, *"I am the way the truth and the life, no one comes to the Father except through me." John...14.1-6*

Copies write c.1949-50 Bible.

A Slice of the Pie

Remembering
the steps in my life

Me at 4 years

It is September 4, 2012

Not remembering, but being told, I was the first born of ten children, a baby girl, 7 lb.'s, 20 inches long, with dad's red curly hair, Elaine to Bill and Mary Py on September 15, 1942, in Roxborough Memorial Hospital, located in the East Falls section of Philadelphia. PA. I was baptized a Catholic, on October 16th same year, in St. Bridget Catholic Church. Oh! It makes me 12 days shy of my 70th birthday; I better get started so I can finish the story before I get *OLD.*

In September of 1948, I had just turned six, mom and I were on the front steps of Corpus Christi Catholic Church one Sunday, while she, and Fr. Kane, were speaking to each other, after the 9:00 AM children's Mass. (Mom always stayed after mass, and would talk the poor priest's ear off), I stood watching the people going and coming. Many of the women seemed and looked very old. I thought to myself, *what would it be like to be* **OLD**? Today I am still wondering.?

I want to state in the very beginning of this story. My reason to do so is because **dates, and time, go back and forth, not in chronological order, and all told is the *truth*.** Our Mother was a devout Catholic. She attended Mass every Sunday. Mom never missed other church services that went on. She belonged to the Catholic Woman's Solidarity, which met every Tuesday evening in our church. She went to the Stations of the Cross on Fridays during Lent. Every other Saturday mom hit the **confessional, whether she needed to confess, or not**. She took each of us, who were seven years and older with her, we had to confessed also, even if we were good and did not sin. My mother just wanted to receive the Sacrament of Penance, now called (*Reconciliation*).

She also went to BINGO at Incarnation church hall, when she had some *dough to play with*. After she retired at age 70, mom attended mass daily. She would walk the nine blocks one way, from 4722 N. 2nd St. to Incarnation Church located at 5th and Lindley Avenues, no matter what the weather conditions were.

On the other hand, dad got to church when we children received our sacraments, also on some Holy Days, and the truth be told, when he was bred, wed, and, dead. That was dad. You had to love him, he was our father, and no matter if he sat out on Sunday, or not. God knows he was a good man and did his best. Mom made sure dad received the Last Rights. I am positive he made it to Heaven.

How many of us, who are alive think about our last day? How about our day of reckoning? Will we be *ready* to meet **Our Lord**, like our mother-grandmother was, when the Lord came to call her home, that Sunday June 11, 1995?

Recollections

At what age can a child start to remember things in the beginning of their life? Most of the early years that we speak of, are hearsay, stories that we were told by parents, grandparents, or other relatives. My true recollection of any of my memories started at about age four. Of course, the Py story began long before dad's and my birth. It starts like all family history does, with our ancestry, and the stories handed down by word of mouth. Now, in this 21st century it is all done on the computer. Just start typing in a little of one's family history, and we can explore our ancestry. You still must have some details, that were passed on to us by a family member, which enables one to search the Internet. I am trying to give as many details to our **family** as I can, so no one can say, *"We were never told anything"*.

My true story, in this book as I recall it, is the start of my dad, and mom's story, the one about their lives, and their ten children. *"A Slice of the Pie"*, is a truth to be shared by our extended family members, and any other interested readers, it is a tale about a lot of, love, laughter, tears, and even, for a better way of putting it *dislikes.* Here it is, as people would say in a **NUTSHELL**, but I say in a **PIE SHELL**. I will start with just a little history of our beginnings. It may be boring to some readers, but not anyone related to the Py's and their clan. I like to get right into **the meat of a book** myself, **so other than a family member (Py and offspring) I will be like the nuns in Catholic School, and give you permission to skip the history, and geography lesson for today; go on read ahead, I won't mind, you can skip the next few pages,** but then you would not want to miss my true tale and the ingredients in the Py- Pie.

*(start about the last paragraph-page 18)

Starting with our dad, the Py, he was half Irish, and French. The Irish with Sir name (Hoban) originated in Kilkenny, Ireland, his French side came from Alsace Lorraine. The French side that married came from border areas to Alsace including Germany. The earliest Py documented to our ancestry is Jean Claude Py, Sr. born c. 1760. His birthplace is unknown, but he was married in Wertheim, which is just north of Mulhouse, Haut Rhin, France in 1791. Through immigration records, some of the earliest Py's that come to the US settled in the Ohio and adjacent Northern PA. area. The family is listed, as being born in Switzerland, the area they came from is right next to Alsace. Some later Py immigrants are recorded as being from France, and others from Germany, but the borders were very fluid over the years. Our documents show we are French, but only on the Py side. Jean Claude, Sr. married Marie Anne Hitter or Heater in Wertheim, Haut, France on January 17, 1791. Jean Claude was a Journalier, (one who works the land), but not his own, he was a tenant farmer. He and Marie had a daughter **Marie Agatha Py** born late October 1791 in Wisenheimer, France and two sons **Jean Claude Py, Jr.** born 1792 in Lauterbach, Haut Rhin, France, and **Nicholas Py** born 1794, in

Neff Breach, Haut Rhin, France **(our line)**. **Jean Claude Py Sr.** died August 16, 1797, when Nicholas was only three years old. Sometime, between Jean's death, and 1822, the three children and their Mother Marie Anne, moved to Mulhouse. **Nicolas Py, Sr. was our three times great grandfather;** he was witness, or godfather to many of his older brother Jean Jr.'s 11 children. So, large families must run in the Py's. My dad, an only child, must have caught the bug. He missed the tie by one. Two of Jean Claude Py's children, immigrated to Mulhouse. Great-great grandfather Nicholas Py, Jr. was born November 28, 1823 also in Mulhouse, France. He met, fell in love, and married Marie Anne Kimmel on December 3rd, 1860 in Mulhouse. Marie was born April 17, 1835 in Schon au, Bavaria. To my knowledge they had only one child **Alphonse Py, (dad's middle name)** born March 11, 1868 in Mulhouse. It is unknown if he had any other siblings. **Alphonse** was our **great grandfather**; He immigrated to the US, arriving July 17, 1893, and registered Philadelphia as his destination. He listed his occupation as **"rabotter-de-far"** it sounds French to me, but what do I know this, *all-American girl*? After I did some research, it is *French,* and means **iron** or **metal worker**. Great grandfather met Emily Vest also from Mulhouse. She lived on Main Street, in Manayunk, and he also lived in Manayunk as well, at 212 Center St. They were married April 19, 1894. The happy couple had two children, Joseph Francis Py (his title is Medical Doctor) he was born on October 7, 1895 he is our Great Uncle, and **Carl Alphonse** Py, born July 10, 1897, is our **granddad**. To my knowledge the both boys were born in the Manayunk section of Philadelphia, PA. Oddly enough when the great grandfather, Nicholas, immigrated to the states, the occupation in 1800's for the Pys was **metal workers**. Dad followed in this trade. Our father, **William Alphonse** was born January 26, 1920 to Carl A. Py (just twenty-three years old) and Mary Dorothy, nee Hoban, our *Meme;* she was nineteen when she became a young mother. Both our Py grandparents were American born.

I was told, I could not say grandmom, and hearing everyone call her Mary, I started to do the same, but Meme came out, and she remained that to all her ten Py grandchildren until the day she went home to be with God, and her son Billy, in Gods Mansion. Dad died before his mother. Parents are not supposed to burry a child. But as we all know; life and death are in the hands of the Lord our God.

Carl A. Py left Mary Py and her child Billy, while dad was just a very young baby. I do not know what lead to the separation, there are speculations that Uncle Bob stated, but I am unable to comment. Carl remarried, and had a son, Robert Claude Py, (Bobby) in 1931. Bobby was dad's half-brother, (unbeknown to my father for over twenty some years, I was also told the couple had a daughter, Margaret (Peggy) dad's half-sister, he never knew of her. Maybe they just met in Heaven. She died this year, 2018. Funny how they all keep secrets., isn't it? I hope dad met his sister in Heaven.

Bobby and Peg

Carl and new wife

Carl A. Py my Grandfather died April 24, 1943 at the early age of forty-six. I am sure we never met. He is buried in Lawnview Cemetery, in

Philadelphia, PA. I hope to visit the cemetery someday, **maybe in the Spring of my life, at his gravesite,** when nature wakes up, and I have a need to meet one of the two grandfathers I never knew.

I met Uncle Bobby, Carl Py's second son, when I was about twelve. This is how I remember the legend. Bobby was dad's half-brother; my father found this out upon Bob's arrival one Friday evening early September, c1955. As I was just leaving for my Girl Scout meeting, a young man showed up on our front porch, he told Mom he was Bobby Py dad's half-brother. "Shock" plus more was the look on our faces. He looked to be in his twenties. Bob stated he needed a place to stay for a day or two until he got **back on his feet.** Our newest uncle had been living in **Fairmount Park**, not the section of, **but in the park**. I guess there were homeless people back in the   50's too.? Dad received this information via mom by a phone call over to his work. Dad came right home, **which was out of the norm for a Friday night.** I guess curiosity was more important than a beer, and a card game. Dad met his half-brother for the first time, and invited him to stay for dinner, and a **short** stay until

Uncle Bob could find a rooming house, or another place to live; so, this part of my story goes. Mom, and dad had seven slices of our Py by then, and the pie tin was getting crowded, if I am correct, mother had another bun in the oven, the baby was due in late November. They **really** needed an extra mouth to feed, let alone one more to bed down at this time in their lives. My parents never turned anyone away, so **Uncle Bobby** was the first guest of many, to stay at our so-called Bed & Breakfast. Back in the early 50's, (dad called it "Pys Wharf") I do not think anyone had thought of that type of lodgings yet, if so it would have been for the very upper crust. Not our Pie Crust. **Uncle Bobby's** bed was our only couch. **He remained off his feet, and on that sofa, much longer than two days.** Weeks, more like a month, and a half went by, when Mom finely put her foot down. I **think it was DOWN? Maybe it was** **up?**

Family Photo of 8 children, mom and dad, Richie's arm is all the camera captured off dad's right side. Richie always seemed to be out of the lens As you can see, our only sofa was full enough, without it having to be a bed

I guess Uncle Bobby got a sore butt? One morning as I left for school he was snugly tucked asleep" *on his bed"* in our small living room. At noon time when I returned home from school for lunch, I asked for the uncle, mom told me "*He moved on.* "This was fine with me; I was finally able to sit on the sofa, and not the old solid wood floor. There were ten of us including my parents at the time, and our little tails were sore from sitting on the uncarpeted living room floor. Mother would need her seat on the couch to feed the new baby girl, Kathleen, the eighth slice of our Pie. Uncle Bob would call occasionally, and let us know of his progress, and who's "Bed & Breakfast" he had found lodging at. Uncle Bob started his road trip. He found a job and married his girlfriend Patricia; they had four children during their marriage, all girls who helped us carry our Py heritage into the future. Time went on, and we lost track of Uncle

Bob, until about seventeen years ago c.2001.

My niece, Nicole Py our (Brother Bill's daughter), an art teacher, or technical aid had to retrieve some art work for the school she taught at. She went to an Art Archives to pick up some portraits. She had to, sign her name for the release of the items. After writing in **Nicole Py**, the director at the desk asked her if she knew William Alphonse Py. *"Of course,"* Nicole said, *"he **was** my father's da*d and my grandfather."* The person at the sign-out desk was no other than Uncle Bobby Py. We had a reunion up in Reinhold's PA. at my brother Joe's home. Nicole invited Uncle Bob, who met almost all the ten slices of the pie, their spouses, and about thirty of our growing family. Our family's size overwhelmed him. Uncle Bob had eight children by then. Margaret his sister had ten children, as I stated in the history lesson, **most of the Py's had large families;** it must have been the **French** in them. Oh Lula! Bob brought us photos, and a lot more of our family history that helped me fill in some of the blanks at the beginning of this story. Uncle Bob and Dad's father, Carl, died when he was just forty-six years of age. Mom always said, "All charitable deeds get rewarded. "Thanks mom, and dad, for lending a stranger complementary room and board for a while. It was worth it in the years   to   come.

There is one last part to our Uncle Bobby's story I must end with. When I was a twelve-year-old girl, I saw a young man who wanted to be something in life, but at the time he did not seem to have any direction. This of course, was my perception. Well! just recently I found an article about Robert C. Py, it went like this- "**Py**' was born in Philadelphia in 1931. A product of the Great Depression, his early **art** was influenced by the Ash Can School of Art of that time, led by Sloan, Hoper, Henri and others, in the late 50's he moved to **New Orleans** where he fell in love with, and was influenced by the **Jazz scene**. It was during the three years stay in New Orleans he met, and painted with Paul Fleagal, a noted Cubist of the time. He learned to manipulate Form, and Space, therefore bringing a higher level of intensity to his ART. He then moved to the magic of **San Francisco**, where he painted two Jazz Album covers for Columbia Records called, **"Space Traveler**", and" **Waiting for the Rain**" Many of Py's paintings can be found in collections around the world. Robert Carl Py has won many awards. Though influenced by the iconic Cubist Movement, spearheaded by, Georges

Braque's and Pablo Picasso....Py works all the, "ISISISM" to express himself, and get his point across" You may be able to check on line for a photo, and a title of one of his works **"Bourbon Street" 1959** .Who would have thought? From homeless in the park to a sofa at 4722 N. 2nd Street, Philadelphia, PA, and on to BOURBON STREET, New Orleans, LA., and then to San Francisco, CA. I wonder what type of transportation he used. What rail line he traveled? If money was tight, it could have been the Hobo Express. Way to go Uncle Bob. **Note:** Uncle Bob died in September 2016 and never had the chance to read my book.

I skipped away from my story, but this was a Miracle of Love, & Art, that I had to put a finish to his story, and Bobby's piece of a different type of PIE -Py

Continuing with the occupations of the Py's, and the rest of our ancestry, Dad was a sheet metal worker, one of the **best** Heliarc Welders in Philadelphia. Mom was born January 22, 1920, to Mary M. Walsh, and John J. Weldon. My grand mom Weldon traveled alone from Castlebar, Mayo, Ireland (3,126 miles) to the United States, when she was only eleven years old. I do not know anything about our great grand-mother "Mary Walsh"; she died giving birth to my grand mom. An aunt, a sister to Michael Walsh our great grandfather, raised grand mom. Michael Walsh, at age thirty-five left Ireland for the United States, just after he buried his wife. I don't know my great grandmothers madden name, or where in Ireland she was born. Michael married Margaret Dolor, she too was born somewhere in Ireland, but both Michael, and she met in the United States; they had two children a boy, Tom Walsh, Uncle Tom born March 13, 1908, and Helen Walsh (Nan) borne in 1911 right before grand arrived in the states, Mary M. Walsh now had a family, a half brother and sister. When my grandmother arrived from Ireland to the States in c.1911, by passage on one of the Irish ships, her father and new family welcomed her at the docks in Philadelphia.

At age 18 Mary Walsh, met and married our grandfather John J. Weldon, c.1918-19, it was sometime just after he returned home from "The Great War". The named changed to The First World War, after the beginning of The Second World War. We only have one photo of our grandfather. The photo of them on the next page was taken on their wedding day., the date is unknown.

The grandfather was ten years older than Mary Walsh our grandmother. John J., like grandmom he was Irish and from a free state. I was unable to find out what part of Ireland grandfather came from. A lot of Weldon's were from Liverpool, England, but grandmother stated he was from Ireland, and was most sure he was as Irish as she was. Ancestry.com states he was from Ireland, so it is confirmed. They rented their first home at 2057 N. 21st St. for $30.00 a month. Beside the oldest four

children that lived in the 21st street home, they took in a border, Michael Hannagan he also came to the US, from Ireland in 1911. My Grandfather helped get him employment at Radio Mfg. Co, this is info I got from the ancestry.com website. No other credentials about the grandfather were ever located. He died seventeen years into their marriage c1935; his burial place is unknown to us. John J. Weldon did not have a will, or any possessions to put in one. Mary Weldon, now a widow with six children, ages fifteen (mom) to a six-year-old (Uncle Tommy), had a nervous breakdown, and was placed in a mental health unit of an unknown hospital for about a year. Great Aunt Helen nee (Walsh) Bremser, Mary's half- sister helped take care of the younger siblings. My six-year-old Uncle Tommy was placed in St. Joseph's Home for boys. Mary T. Weldon (Mom) took a part time job working after school and weekends to help with the bills. Mother was able to continue her education at John W. Hallahan Catholic High School for Girls, where she excelled as an honor student and, graduated. Mom's siblings were our Uncle John, Aunts Dot, Peggy, Helen and, my "**Uncle Tommy**". When grandmom was well enough she returned home, at which time she was able to cope with the death of her loving John and continued raising her family. In those days, times were very trying.

Mother and dad met in c.1940 at the Liedertafel a German Club in North Phila. They married June 6, 1941. By the way, I thought mom always acted older than dad, being his senior by four days. Mom always wore a **housedress,** or should I say a **maternity dress**, but in our eyes, she wore the **pants** in the family. Dad died in the Veterans Hospital in Philadelphia, PA on January 26, 1976 of wounds and other conditions, related to WWII, while serving in the United States Army. It was his fifty-six birthday, and his death day. What a wonderful birthday gift, to be able to meet the Lord our God and join Him at His Heavenly Banquet. *Well!* There may have been a stopover in Purgatory before he got his seat, and beer mug, at the Lords table. Mom was just fifty-six years old herself, with some teenagers to chase after; she had to pay Catholic High School fees, for at least the last two children. Mom's father died when she was only fifteen years old. My sister Jeannie was sixteen, when we lost dad. *I am sure mom recalled her own father's death again.* Mother had been back in the work force for a while before dad died, so she did have a small income, but not enough to maintain a family, and household bills. Mother was too young to get widows benefits from Social Security; she had to be age sixty to apply, (what a bust this was, for a person with no spouse to help pay the bills). There was *"a Silver Lining"* to the last day of dad's life. I will explain as I continue to tell my story. All the above was a brief history that I was told, or started to witness, and the rest of this story, I lived, and learned, as I grew into adulthood.

The beginning, and 1st steps in my life, and my memories, I do not know when I started crawling, walking, or even talking., (although I have not stopped yacking since) Mom did not keep a memory book, and my parents **never told us much of family matters.** *After my birth, until I was 3 or 4 years old, there is not much of my story to tell. Mom never revealed much of anything.* I do know, at twelve years old, I found out about life, and a little of the **birds & bees** stuff on my own, and my mother's youngest sister, Aunt Helen (Weldon) Smith, helped me handle mother, and my new *"friend"*. Woman never spoke about those important personal topics. I wonder if they do now?

Mother told me she worked at Beaux Cigars, while my father had been picked in the first draft to enter World War II; he was stationed in Italy during the war. Grand mom Weldon and her five young adult children, three aunts, and two uncles took care of me while my parents were serving our country. Mom was in a cigar factory doing men's work, and dad was dodging bullets at the front line in Sicily, and Giada Italy. He was in Lt. Gen. Mark Clark's 5th Army 45th Division with Oklahoma, and Texas soldiers; I often wondered how dad, with a Philadelphia twang understood the southern, and western drawl of his new comrades. While *OVER THERE,* during the very cold and snowy winter, he was diagnosed to have had frostbitten feet, and the sounds of the guns firing damaged his ears. I now wonder if he also had **flash backs**, and **trauma** from that horrible war. As the good young trooper, he was, he never complained. Dad spent time in a military hospital in Italy to heal his feet. While he was recuperating, his friend, and Army Captain George Berg, would come, take him from the hospital in his Army jeep, they toured the area, and would stop in a little bakery to pick up fresh breads. Dad always had American rations (Hershey Chocolate Bars) with him; he would hand out the candy bars to the children of the owner of the bake shop. (It is now a Café, or Bar). I will give you my brother Joe's version of this tale later as the story continues. After dad was discharged from the hospital he would be back out on the front line. Dad never put in a claim to the Veterans Administration for the health problems he had endured during the war. Much later in the beginning of dad's 55th year

1975, I met a World War I veteran, Charles Gossner. I knew him through the Cub Scout Troop 316, that my four boys belonged to, oops I just left the cat out of the bag. During the time my sons were in the Scout troop, at St. Ambrose Parish, C Street and Roosevelt Blvd., he inquired about my father. Mr. Gossner was an older man, who belonged to the American Legion Post and the VFW in the Olney section of *Philadelphia*. *He* took an interest in my **dad's history** back to dad's honorable discharge in 1944 and submitted a claim to the VA in my father's name. January 26th, 1976 the day of dad's death, mom received a check from the Federal Government in the amount of $16,000.00, for prorated disability pay dad should have gotten at the time of his full honorable discharge from the United States Army. The funds were issued to William A. Py. Dad did not have a **WILL**, not many people did in those years. (**It is important to have a WILL, no matter how young or old you are**). Even if you are penniless, a **WILL** is a necessity. The hospital administrator took my dying fathers hand, and put an X on the check, it was than notarized. Mother was told by the administrator to rush to her bank and deposit the government check. She hopped into a cab, did as directed, and returned to the now Michael J. Crescenz VA hospital to find out dad passed away ten minutes after the time stamped on the bank deposit slip. The fact that there was no Will, the check would have had to be returned to the government. WOW! How about that windfall for my mom? Thank you, Lord, for watching over our mom in her time of need.

MY   FANCY   STEPS

I know I was one of the first girl GOGO dancers in a bar, at age four Great Uncle Charlie Bremser my grandmom' s half-brother in-law would take me to Kane's Bar on the corner of 22nd and Westmorland Streets in North Philadelphia, there he would stand me up on the bar, and tell me to dance to and fore, (TAP) that is; so as I promenaded up, and down while the juke box played a tone, all the male patrons would give me quarters. This was great, by the end of a month of Saturday's I earned more money than a paper carrier. If I only knew then, what the going rate for a GOGO girl would be in the 21st century? I must laugh! Oh well that was then, many years ago, and I never had an hour glass body like the dancing girls have today. Uncle Charlie was just enjoying his little niece and showing me off. Great Uncle Charlie was Captain of the Dick

Crain String Band. The band was formed and named after a man who owned a small department store at 28th & Allegheny, Dick Crain's .

Dad a self-taught musician played the banjo (that heirloom is located at Joe & Ruth Py's home, it has not been played since 1976. Dad also play the Bells (Xylophone), he too was in the string band, along with his old army captain George Berg, who play the harmonica and an accordion. (Moira my Lynch-Hurst granddaughter is enjoying playing the Bells and other Percussion instruments). I can remember Great Aunt Helen (Nan), and her two children took me to many New Year's Day parades, just to see them march up Broad Street. By the time the String Bands hit the judging stands at City Hall, it would be dark, and very cold. We did not mind, we had hot chocolate, and our love of the parade to keep us warm. "OH, Those Golden Slippers."

The year Uncle Charlie was getting ready to retire from the band, the Dick Crain string band placed third in the music, and marching competition, and first place Captain's prize was awarded to my Uncle Charles Bremser. What a tremendous way to end his many years of string band days, and to start the New Year. The Bremser children's names were the same as the parents, only it was Little Helen, and Charlie, Jr. Who, by the way Charlie was a dead ringer for Mickey Rooney the movie star, size, and all. I do not know why Great Aunt Helen was nick named Nan, but it suited her fine. Parents named their children after themselves, a special family member, or even a Saint. Now day's babies are named after movie, TV, or sports stars, sometimes their first name is a last name. I still cannot figure that out! There will never be a better time than the days during the (40's 50',s & 60's) when I was g rowing up. I only remember a little of Great Uncle Tom Walsh, Nan's brother, grand's half- brother. Our family would stop in to visit him and his family, while we were on our way to aunt Nan's on Westmoreland St. near 20th. he lived only two blocks from his sister's home, we would have refreshments, he would tease me, and call me his **Peachy Pie**, or **Cutie Pie**. I would laugh and play while the adults did their normal socializing, then it would be time to leave. I think he was sickly. I would hear them say "he has the sickness"?

Years later, the week before Valentine's Day, I remember it was February 8, 1982, Great Aunt Helen (Nan) had stopped by her friend's Mrs.

Feeley's house, after coming from buying Valentine day cards for the family. Her friend greeted her, with sorrow in her eyes, "Nan" she said, "*I am so sorry about your brother Tom*", Nan said, "*Oh, I must call him and see how he is feeling*", Nan asked "*may I use your phone?*" My aunt's friend told Nan, "*Tom died about a half hour ago*". Aunt Nan sat on the end of Mrs. Feeley's sofa; **she put her hand on her heart and she died too.** Heaven must have had a choir of Cherubim's and Seraphim's dancing and shooting love arrows that Valentine's Day. It was not a loving time for any of our family. Instead of Hearts, Chocolates, and Flowers for Saint Valentine's Day, that year, we had **broken hearts and funeral flowers.** In telling this part of the story, **(The *Steps of My Life*),** I jump from early childhood to adulthood, back and forth. It's the way I remember the circumstance's, and the connections to early memories, and what happened through the later parts of my life, so stay with me, as I go from an innocent child to a mature adult.

I was three years old when I received a tricycle for Christmas from no other than the man in the **Red Suit**, and mom told me I could ride it in the cellar. (Today it would be a basement or reck-room). When I was about four and a half, they cut me loose and let me ride it outside. Bad News! Living only one very long block, and across a major four lane highway (**Hunting Park Ave**.) from my Great Grand-pop William Hoban, a retired Philadelphia Firefighter, I decided I would ride over and visit him. We lived at 3103 N. 28th St. at Clearfield, in Philadelphia, and Great Grand- father lived on the far side of Hunting Park Ave, at Napa St. Pop Hoban lived in the big corner property. Thank God for my guardian angel, "Helen" I made it to safety. (Photo I am the child in navy blue, outside Pop Hoban's home with Delores Hildebrand, in gray she is a distant cousin, we were almost four years old, at the time of this photo. I am still trying to locate Delores on Face Book, but no luck so far.

I am **looking at you kid"**

With a big smile on my face and love in my heart, I rang pop's door bell, my Great Aunt Margaret, Meme's sister answered the door.

Looking behind me for mom or dad she went into shock. *"How did you get here"*? *"My bike'* I answer with a smile on my face. All I saw on Aunt Margaret's face was a big frown, and in a matter of minutes a phone call was made from the party line, (for the younger generation a party line is your phone service, but you share it with two or four other people on the same line) depending on your ability to pay the phone company, you shared a two or four line. Pop Hoban had a two liner. I believe he had a lot of money., only a child would say that. It seemed like it was only seconds when my father was at the door to escort me and the bike home. We left without a soda or even a pretzel. No words were spoken on the walk back to 28th Street. When we arrived home, I did get something, it was my very first spanking. It was the first of the only two I ever received in my life. Well that tricycle was put back in the cellar for posterity, only until the Christmas that followed. They told me, if I was a **good girl**, maybe *Santa* would bring a new two-wheeler with training wheels, like the kind my friends had, my tricycle would be saved for my baby brother Billy. I was surprised that Christmas of 1947 because there was a shiny red and white bike with red, white, and blue streamers on each handlebar, and a bell, it was left hiding in the kitchen of our four-room home. (Oh, we did have an indoor bathroom making it five rooms). I was told, "It's winter now, so you will have to wait until it gets warmer to be able to take it out to sidewalk". This was ok with me. I spent a lot of time from Christmas morning until about the middle of February 1948 practicing riding in that cold cellar. One Monday night a man came to our home, he had a black book in his hand. He and dad talked for a while, and then we all went to the lower level. The stranger proceeded to take the bike **Santa** brought me for Christmas." **NO!**" I cried, "**Santa** *gave it to me*". He said, "*I am sorry little girl*" and up the steps he went with the bike, and the **black** book. I cried for a long time, mother and dad said, **"everything would be OK."** How could they tell me this? It was a long time before I found out it was not **Santa** who brought it. They purchased the bike at Lemans Department Store on Market Street, in downtown Philadelphia. People were able to put a down payment on items and pay a set amount of cash each week until it was paid off. A debt collector would come out to your home once every two weeks, take the cash, and mark the amount paid in the **BLACK BOOK**. Being only five, and not knowing the financial problems my young parents were having, I was at a loss as to why my ride was being, for a better word **repossessed**. Yes, I did get over the loss of that bike. By the time spring came, I guess I also forgot my first spanking. Not too long after my bike trip to my great grandfather's house, dad asked me to go to the corner store and get a loaf of bread. No one needed cash, back then because all the families ran a tab at the local grocery store, they called it THE *BOOK*. Oh, there was that word again, (**BOOK**) or, put it on the EYE until payday. Our street was a very long block from Clearfield to Alleghany Ave. and I was playing with the kids. So, I saw a boy, a little older than I, Eddie Ward, his dad drove for Yellow Cab Co, at the time they lived a few houses down from us. I said. "Eddie if you go down to the corner store and get my dad a loaf of bread he will give you a penny." Wow! a penny was worth two pieces of candy back in 1948, (*now people drop pennies on the ground and just leave them there*); so, Eddie got the bread and took it to dad; he stood there with his hand out for the reward. He got the promised penny, and I got, you guessed it, another spanking from my father. I finely learned my lesson. I never again received as much as a scolding. I must mention my backside never had pain again, except for the time we met *Uncle Bobby Py,* when we had to give up our couch, so he would have somewhere to sleep. Oh, I forgot about the **hemorrhoid's** got them after my child birthing days. Thank you, God, for my conscience, and for the knowledge of not doing wrong, this my parents instilled in me at a very young age. I never regretted corrective criticism.

While dad was overseas helping defend our country and mom working at the cigar factory; I spent the first three years of my life living at grand mom Weldon's house. During all the off and on stays there, it was my **Uncle Tom** who had to keep an eye on me, he was about eight or nine years older then I. It was as if I had a big brother. With all Grand had to do, Tom was put in charge of occupying me. Tommy took me everywhere. He belonged to a group of boys all his age, they were not happy to have a girl hanging around them all day. The fact that I was only a little kid really dampened their style. But, it was like this, either I got into their group, or Tom would be out. No VOTE took place I was in, and that was that. When dad was discharged from the U.S. Army, and Mom stopped working, because the servicemen, who returned home from overseas needed their jobs back, Mom was now "a stay at home mom", so I was sent back to our house on 28th Street, full time. I spent less time at grandmom' s house, and I missed running with my Uncle Tom and his friends even though I was very young.

My Schooling

I attended Whittier Public School for kindergarten; it still sits on the corner of 27th and Clearfield Streets. Miss. Hamburg was the teacher, I thought the name Py was different, but Hamburg? O well, nothing exciting happened that year, as I took my first baby step away from mom, for a half day. However, First Grade in Corpus Christi Catholic School, located at 28th and Wishart Streets was a different story. The first day of school, and all I could think of as I approached the front door, was: who is this person in the long black gown with a big white bib at her neck? I could not see if she had hair, or ears behind the strange head piece. I do know one thing, she had eyes in back of her head, all nuns did. "Mom please don't leave me with this person". Well she did, and I met Sister Mary Ellen, a Sister of Saint Joseph. My year was moving right along, until one day, I was late getting back to school from lunch. I had vegetable soup that day, and mother had put one of her soiled aprons on me, so not to mess up my clean uniform, it was much too big for me. I must have had a hole in my chin that afternoon, because there was more soup on the apron than in my tummy. "Hurry" mom said, "the bell will ring, and you will be late". I quickly put on my coat, out the door, and crossed 28th Street. I ran down one block to the school, just made it before the bell rang. We filed into the cloak room to hang up our coats, and there it was, **the dirty apron**. I would not go into the classroom. I stood with my coat on, holding it closed, and cried like a baby. Sister tried to get me to remove my coat. I clung to the buttons. The coat was not coming off. Sister called mom, and asked her to come down to school, to see if she could find out what my problem was. **Mom could fix any problem**. I whispered in her ear about the messy apron under my coat, and quickly she removed the coat, scooped up the apron and, I was on the road to recovering from my revolting disaster. When I think about my crying over a silly matter like that, it reminds me of a little girl in my class, her name was Anna Marie Cone, I can still see her to this day. She cried all day every day. Anna Marie's mother had a nice clean handkerchief pinned to her uniform all the time, just for the tears. I often wondered why she cried so much. I never had the chance to get to know her. I finished first grade in the spring of 1949, along with all my good friends. We were looking forward to another wonderful summer, like the last summer in1948. Only to find out, that was not going to happen. On the last day of school, when I returned home, there was a big sign hanging on the porch. **FORECLOSURE** it read, of course I didn't know the meaning of the word, *"Mom"* I ask, *"What does that sign mean?"* *"We are moving"* I was told, my Brother Bill, Mom, Dad our new baby sister Patty, and yours truly. We were going to stay with grandmom Weldon, along with Uncle John J. Jr. Aunts Dot, Peggy, Helen, and my Uncle Tom, a dog name (Skippy) and, nine cats, some of them were new kittens. This was a temporary move, *just until we get back on our feet* she said. Sounded like I mentioned something like that before? Oh, by the way Mother would have named Patty, Josephine Agnate, because she was born on St. Joseph's day, March 19th. I **begged** her not to name my new baby sister Josephine, I said *"Mom, we could name her after St. Patrick", his day is March 17th*. I won that battle, but as far as the move, I had no say. No one asked me if I wanted to move. It was a done deal.

We were packing and getting ready for a new life. *I could not let this move sink into my brain or aching heart.* I was still planning my summer, like the one I had last year c.1948. Back in the day c.1947-1949 children young as maybe, three and a half, four, five and six, could be left out to play and wander the neighborhood streets. Not too far, about a two or three block radius. There was never fear that something bad would happen to the children. In this 21st Century the children are keep under protective care until about eleven years old. What a changed world we live in. **NOTE** Adults in N.E Philadelphia aren't even safe out alone at night. (Aug. 5, 2014; woman jogger strangled in Penny Pack Park) No Suspects. In the end it turned out to be murder, by her husband. But the truth is the streets and parks are not safe in the evenings any more. C.2018

In our N. Philadelphia neighborhood, we had the public swimming pool (we called it the Shimmies) located at 27th and Indiana. There were two waiting rooms, capacity for about 30 people in each. One for girls with a sign that read (Bathing Caps & Dry Suits Required) the other room was for boys. I do not know if there was a sign in the boys, since girls were not allowed in that one back then, now days is a total different story? The swim would be every hour on the hour. The two waiting rooms would open at 8:00 AM and all heck would break out, kids running, yelling, and jumping in and out of the swimming pool, on the early swim the water was always cold. It got warmer as each swim hour was over. I *hope it was the sun that warmed the water*? At exactly five minutes before each hour, the whistle would blow. Everyone would exit a rear door onto 27th Street. You could not go back for another swim until you bathing suit was completely dry. Some children had a second suit. They must have been rich kids; they would quickly change into the dry suit, lay the wet one in the sun to dry, run to the entrance, and get ready for the next swim. The less fortuned children, like me, would enter the Whittier playground adjacent to the pool, we would hop on the swings and hope while swinging higher and higher the air would dry our suits, so we could go back to the pool in an hour. What fun I had with all my little friends. On the corners of Indiana Avenue and 27th to 28th streets there was The Public Water Works, now (Aqua PA) it had a huge pipe yard. It seemed like some of the pipes were as big as a house to us kids. They were all shapes and sizes with holes some on the sides and some in the top. The water company had a guard, in full uniform with a time clock checker. We would run and play hide and seek in this imaginary Kingdom of Pipes. Jim Durkin just called it The Pipes. But watch out for the guard. If he could catch you, you would be taken home to your parents, and guess what we could expect. Most of us were the first Blue Ribbon Track Runner's, we never got caught. How simple life was. I had so many friends in my young world on 28th Street. I can still remember most of the names. Going down the street toward Allegheny Ave., was the Jewish family right next door, Mr. and Mrs. Pencil, their son Sonny was my friend and their daughter Edna was the one who baby sat my brother Billy and I, when my parents had the cash, and the chance to step out for an evening. On those special nights, mom and dad would get all dolled up, and right before they would head out, they would put Billy, and I in their big bed. Mom would say our good night prayer, and both my parents would pull the blankets up to our necks, tucking us in and saying *"Good night you little bunny rabbits, be good for Edna. We will see you in the morning."* Somehow or other we, my brother and I would wake up in our own beds. It took me a while to figure   that   one   out.

My memory of the old neighborhood and my friends from sixty-five years ago is like it was yesterday. Here is the street line up, down from the Pencils was good old Eddie Ward, Marline High her parents had the first TV. Ginger Dempsey, Joey Fioca, Kathleen Tyrell, and the Durkins, who at the time lived at the end of the block, Judy was the daughter's name maybe a younger brother Jimmy? (I recently in Nov. 2014 ran into a Jim Durkin at the Central Association of the Miraculous Medal Shrine in Germantown. It was the same little brother of Judy. (How small this world is to reunite 65 years later; of course, he did not remember me, but I remembered him; now he and his wife Joanne, and I have become e-mailers, and all four of us got together in Florida in February 2015). Jim died April 17, 2017. I got a call from Joanne just a few weeks ago. I am now getting back to the corner of 28th and Clementon Street was a Soda Fountain and candy store, owned by the Mc'Ques. Going down Clementon Street was Nancy Mottson and her brother, (or it could be the McGonigal's) boy?) I can't remember his name, but I can still see him, tall, thin, with a crop of curly reddish hair, as Irish as Patty's Pig he was. I thought he was handsome, can you imagine a six-year-old thinking that? Well I did. On the other side of that street was the Healey Family, lots of kids in that house, maybe eight? Joey was my friend, but it seems he was always being punished for something or other, mom would say "*I don't want you with Joey*" but I did play over there with him; till he go the ring worm. I guess that was contagious, she demanded obedience of me.   At the end of that block, on the corner at 29$^{th.}$ St. was a Bar back than it was called a Taproom). This one had the old fashion saloon half swinging doors, like the kind in the cowhand movies. Sometimes, my dad would stop in that Taproom on his way home from work. If time got away from him, which happened quite often throughout dad's life. Mom would send me over to the bar, to remind him dinner was almost ready. I would crawl under the swinging doors to see if he was there. Yep, there he was standing at the bar, with his foot on the brass rail. Dad always saw me under those doors, he must have known I would be there looking for him, he would call me in for a pop (soda). The ice filled glass, with cola made the drink so delicious, on those sizzling summer afternoons. I also forgot why I was sent there. We would get home just a little later than mom expected, she would be upset, but dad knew how to smooth her over. Across the street, cattycorner from our house was a steep hill at Clearfield and 28th to 29th streets. The field was and is called, Cahill Field. Roman Catholic High School Boys would play Football there. But we kids also played on the hill outside the field. All Summer long we could take big pieces of cardboard and pretend they were sleds. This was all well and good until I slid off my imaginary sled, cut the top of my right leg. Dad was called home from work and I was taken to Roxborough Memorial Hospital for 12 stitches. That was the end of the fun on Cahill's hill for me. I still have the scar. Visible or not, some scars never disappear, like the one I received, with the notice of the moving away from my Swampoodle days, (that was the name of our neighborhood) my time there was running out. In my young mind, my life was over. They were taking me away from everything, and everyone I knew. I was devastated and didn't understand what was happening to our family in 1949. The day the moving van came, all my friends were gathered around watching our things being packed into the truck, and we were in the way of the movers. Dad said, *"Go play, get lost, we have a lot to do before we can leave."* LEAVE? LEAVE! That word hurt so badly. He gave us a dollar to share. We purchased a lot of soda and candy at McQue's, after the owner gave us the third degree, asking, *"Where did you get this dollar young lady?"* *"My dad, he is moving you know?"*, *"Oh he is, is he?"* said Mr. McQue, I said *"Yep look for yourself,"* I pointed to the moving van. *"OK"* said the old man, *"Here are your goodies."* As he smiled, and handed me the bags, he held the last bag back, and asked *"And now, just where would your dad be going?"* in his Irish brogue, *"Do you know?"* I looked up at the proprietor, and just surged my shoulder **as if I were not part of the move**, with that being said, I told my friends, *"Let us go to the Kingdom of the Pipes."* Off we went, to climb in and out of the huge pipes, we hid from the guard, and had such fun laughing, and enjoying the treats. Time went by fast, it was getting late, and my playmates started to disappear one by one. Eddie Ward was the last to go, he said *Come on now, let us go home,"* *"**NO**"* was my reply, he left, and I just sat there alone in that big pipe, gripping the empty brown bags that held our treats, it seemed like it was forever. I did not have ***forever***, only these last few ***moments***, and ***memories***. My forever days were over. Finally, I heard the guard, and dad's voices calling, *"Elaine"*, it was getting dark and I was afraid to come out, of my safe, and oh so happy world. I did not know this was the beginning of another step in my life. Dad calls out to me again, I stepped out of the pipe, and he took my hand, hugged me, and said, *"Everything will be okay honey."* Okay, I heard that so many times before. In my young heart, and mind, I **wondered**? We walked home to 3103 N. 28th Street for the last time.

Our first move, Grand mom here we come

We arrived, all five of us, in early June 1949 to Grand mom's house somewhere in the 2300 block of N. Chadwick Street in North Philadelphia. It was just in time for mom to survey the area for a new school, so I could start second grade while we would be staying with her mother and siblings. My new school would be Our Lady of Mercy, located at Broad and Susquehanna Avenue. This was going to be an interesting change in my life. In first grade, I would cross one street to get to my classroom. Now I had to walk three blocks from Chadwick to Broad; we were close to Lehigh Ave, then I would hike seven more blocks down Broad Street, to the school at Susquehanna Avenue. As the saying goes, (do a dry run), we did a long walk to test it out. Ouch! my poor feet. No money for a bus, and no car. Mother stated, *"You shall walk to school", the walk will do you good"*. Another done deal, I would be turning seven in September, beginning a new grade in a new school, so far from my old home on 28th Street, and all my friends. This was not good for me, so I thought at the time.

In this world life goes on and a little girl almost seven does not have much input in the decisions, and sacrifices her parents had to make to survive. I did get a small rainbow and a pot of gold, at the bottom with this temporary move. I was back in the fold with my old pal Uncle Tommy, and his now teenage friends. It was fine with me.

But his friends were another story. Time passed, and they adapted again. We were lucky to live near Shibe Park, where the Fighting Phil's also known as **THE WHIZ KIDS**, played professional baseball. We had a huge parking business going. The older boys would stand out by the ballpark and direct cars to side streets where we had been saving parking spaces for the ticket holders. We used orange crates to keep the spots open. The same crates we put skate wheels on to make scooters. The fans would pay us money for finding them a parking space. The closer to the park, the more money we made. I got paid for just being there. I know now, I was short changed, but back with my uncle, and his friends, I was happy. One of the older boys had the use of a car and we would pile in and drive around North Philadelphia. One time they hit a pole and paid me $2.00, not to tell anyone about the slight accident. I wonder now, how they explained the dent in the front of Johnny O'Donnell's dad's car. Sometimes we would walk the railroad tracks down by the old Nabisco Baking Factory, at the time it was located somewhere in North Philadelphia. (**Note:** Nabisco had since moved to a new plant on Roosevelt Boulevard). A few years ago, Kraft purchased the Baking Company, and on September 29, 2015 Kraft closed the plant, and sent the backing to Mexico, leaving six hundred workers unemployed, what a shame. I am getting back to the railroad, if the RR police (Bulls, the uniform cops, or Dicks the plain cloths detectives) would come around we would hide under the R/R trestle. No one would make a sound, while hiding from the law. We thought we were so cool. We forgot that Skippy (the old dog), did not like anyone in uniform. I think about the mail person who had to ward off our dog every day. Well, Skippy would start barking, and we were caught. All of us would be in for a ride home in the Paddy Wagon (a police van with benches in the back on each side). Skippy always ended up in the dog pound, over off Clearfield St, (Woman's SPCA) because he would run away, and he did not have a collar on with a licensed dog tag., so when the dog catchers saw him running loose they would scoop him up with a big net, and he got a ride in the SPCA Patty Wagon . Poor Skippy, he spent more time in the pound than some criminals would spend in the pokey. My Uncle John would go to the pound, and give 50 cents to get the dog out, most of the money was for a dog license, but how many times a year did my uncle have to pay for this license? Someone was making money?   September c. 1949 arrived faster than I wanted it to, and school started. I was off for my morning stroll, and Uncle Tom and his friends were beginning junior year at North Catholic High School for boys. (The Catholic Archdioceses of Philadelphia closed this wonderful school run by the Brothers in 2010). Well I saw less of them when school began. I started Our Lady of Mercy with a sure sense of insecurity in my heart. It was difficult for me to forget the friends I left behind. If something or someone does not affect me, I, until this day block it, or them out. This is how it was for me in the beginning of second grade in my new institute of education. I think the move really influenced my learning in a negative way. I did make two friends, they were identical twins. I cannot remember their names, but they were pretty little girls, with blond hair. Unbeknown to me their father owned, and operated an undertaker business, at 2315 N. Broad St. It was in the basement of a big Brownstone, which was their home. We would walk up Broad Street on our way from school, and one day they invited me in. I had nothing else to do; Uncle Tom was in sports after school, so I accepted. We went through the basement entrance of their home. This was the first encounter I had with death. When great grand pop died, he just was not around anymore, and his chair by the window was just empty. No one told me he went to Heaven, he was just missing! So, in the girls house I saw two very shiny large boxes, and in them were life size dolls, at least I thought they were dolls, I inquired as to what I saw, and the two of them laughed, and told me they were dead people. I was informed of what their father **did for a living, or should I say for the dead?** I was in shock. (as if a seven-year-old could have shock?). I never went back to their home again. I was just a kid, and unfamiliar with death. The next two plus months passed slow for me. Grand mom's house was very crowded, and full of noise. People going and coming in and out of my parents make shift bed room. I was lucky I slept in Aunt Dot's master bedroom. The rest of my family occupied the dining room, which had been turned into sleeping quarters for four. (I often wondered what my parents did with their furnishings from our home in Swampoodle)? Mom said, "*I like sleeping in the dining room, my mom makes her Irish Bread at night, while we try to sleep, but the aroma of bread baking smells so delicious I can't wait to wake up for a piece of it with my morning coffee*" Here is **Grandmom Weldon's Irish Bread Recipe- 4** cups white flour, 1 ¼ cup sugar, 1 tea spoon of baking soda, 3 tea spoons baking powder, a pinch of salt, 1 egg beaten, and added to two cups of butter milk, (she never had the money for butter milk, so she would add 2 table spoons of vinegar to the measure of milk "two cups") to make it like butter milk, ½ box of raisins or a little more. Mix all ingredients together. She would say, "don't have the dough too stiff; add more butter milk to loosen the batter for a moist bread you need a wet batter". She used a cast iron frying pan to bake it in. Always grease and flower the pan and bake it in a 350-degree oven for one hour. Test for doneness with a straw from the **broom**. YUCKY, (Today, there are sprays for the baking pans and thin metal testers) Grand mom never updated her method of making this wonderful recipe; she brought in her head from Ireland. When cool, turn bread out of the pan, and sprinkle with 10 X sugar (White Confection Sugar). I hope you enjoy it as we have, on, Thanksgiving, Christmas, and St. Patrick's Day mornings. It is now a Py, Hopkins, Lynch tradition to have this on the holidays I mentioned.

I could smell the bread baking also, but I loved being around my Aunt Dot, she was a fine, and fancy lady. Long black hair, and her finger nails and toe nails were always polished. She sported all the newest style clothing, and shoes. As I got older, she showed me etiquette, poise, and how to dress fancy. In a lot of ways, I followed all her guidance.

Aunt Charlotte (Tom's wife) Uncle Tom Weldon, (Tan jacket), Aunt Dot, & husband Tim Rossetti, in deep brown suit, in picture below

I kept all Aunt Dot's mentoring, in the back of my head until I was able to afford all of the above. I was about twenty-seven years old, before I could have my nails, and hair done by a professional, occasionally that is. Not able to afford to buy all the modern style clothing. I used the sewing skills my grandmother Weldon, and the nuns at Cardinal

Dougherty High School taught me, I made a lot of my clothes, Halloween costumes for my four sons, and, ten grandchildren to be. I was able to make slipcovers for our old furniture, on that ancient second-hand Singer sewing machine my husband John T. bought me a few years after marriage.

Aunt Dot took me to elegant places, such as DeLulas, and Turin Grata Italian Restaurants, Horn and Hardart's Automat was my favorite of all. She showed me how to sip soup properly from the spoon, (dip the spoon into the soup, and scoop it away from you than bring it to your lips) she also showed me how to twirl the pasta with a spoon on to the fork. "**Never cut your spaghetti**" she would say. We attended the Goldman Theater to see, The Song of the South, with Uncle Remus. The best song was **Zip Pity Do Da**. (a note, last July 2015), while strolling on Ocean City board walk, I heard that song over the loud speaker, and it brought back many good memories. What a wonderful time I had with my aunt. We viewed all the great movies at the Goldman Theater. Some were, Wizard of Oz, and Alice in Wonderland, Snow White, and Cinderella which in a way reminded me of myself. NO, I did not have a nasty step mother or two step sisters, but I did have a Fairy God Mother (**Aunt**

Dot). Grandmom would take all of Dot's ball dress and design a new younger style dress or formal for me to wear to my high school dances. Grand mom made my Senior Prom gown; it was a Cinderella ball gown. No one had anything like it. Poor as we may have been in 1960, I always had an original formal dress for a dance.

My senior prom gown.

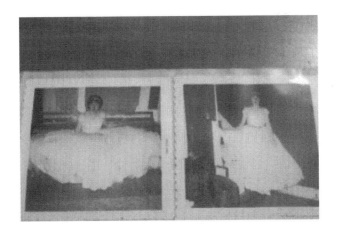

When I was about nine or ten, my aunt, and I would board a train at the old North Philadelphia train station at Broad and Glenwood streets, and head to Atlantic City, every second Thursday in September to see the Miss Ameica pageant parade This ritual went on until I was about13 years old. On one of the trips, we even met BOB HOPE, he kissed my hand. Young as I was, I did not realize his prestige, and stamina until many years later as I continued to watch the Miss America Pageant on Television it was then, I realized his importance. As years past, while he was still the Master of Ceremony, I would just touch my now (older hand) and remember that night on the AC board walk. A smile would be on my face.

My Aunt Dot had a man friend, Bill (Gal they called him), it was short for Gallagher he reminded me of **Gen. Patton**. And he had no time for kids. Dot and he went out on Tuesdays, and Saturdays and he would always take her to New Orleans, LA in February for Fat Tuesday, and all the Margarita festivities. This dating ritual went on for as long as I can remember, I thought Bill Gallagher would ask her to marry him. One night long after I lived on 2nd Street, and spent the weekends at Grands, my aunt came home, and she sobbed all night long, I asked "Aunt Dot, why are you crying?" She said, "Gal is getting married", "Oh can I come to your wedding?" I asked, all she could say was, "He is marrying another lady not me. I was just a young girl; I did not know how to help my aunt, who was always there for me. It was a long time before my aunt went out at night. One-night Aunt Peggy got her to go to a dance at Wagner's Ballroom on Old York Road. Dot met a man, Tim, they dance, dated and she married him late in life. His name was Tim Rossetti, from Pleasantville, NJ. They were about forty-eight to fifty at the time. Tim moved Dot into his home, which was close to AC. I wonder if Dot ever got back to the Atlantic City Boardwalk to see the Miss America Pageant parade. It would have been a short car ride from her home. My aunt did not drive. Maybe she kept that just our special event. I do believe she also took my younger sister Patty to AC once or twice, after I was married. Pat and her husband went a few times to Pleasantville to visit our aunt. The only time I got there, it was too late. It was for her funeral Mass. My favorite aunt, Dot, was the first of my grandmother's children to die, she was only 65 years old, and was diagnosed with the start of Alzheimer's. What a beautiful mind she had in her heyday. She was never blessed with children; I felt God put us together, so I could be her child, *not just her niece*. I was blessed.

While we were staying at Grandmas, she still had the old fashion telephone. When I recall it, the phone sort of reminded me of a doctor's stethoscope. If we needed to make a call, we would pick up the receiver, and make sure no one from your party line was on the other end. If the line was clear, we would proceed to call out. In 1949, and early 50's you only had to dial five numbers to reach the person on the other end. As you know, with today's advance technology land line phones are becoming obsolete. Cell phones, emails, texting, and face book is something no one ever thought of in the early part of the twentieth century. In this fast-paced world, we now live in, it is ten digits to connect to our party, if you even have a land line. Life was easy, slow, and uncomplicated in the days of my youth.

Getting back to my schooling. The first two and a half months of second grade passed. I just made do. Now on the other hand, back living on Chadwick Street, with Grand, my aunts, and uncles were the best days ever. In 1949 people were still feeling strapped, cash wise, with the men returning home from the Second World War and the women getting back in the home. Jobs were still scarce. If you were a family head, you needed a knowledgeable trade to beat out the next man in line for work. My dad was able to land a position at

Mid Vail Steel in the East Falls section of the city, as a welder. He then made enough money, which enabled him to put a down payment on a little bit bigger home in the, I want to say, the lower Olney section of Philadelphia. Some people would argue the issue, and say it was Feltonville and it was, but to me I lived, and grew up in Olney.

Our last big move to Second Street

In November of 1949, we were able to move into our new to us, but older house. I noticed we had a much bigger back yard than our other home on 28th St. this home had a dining room and three bed rooms, our other home was a two-bed room with just a living room and kitchen, a tiny home for a very small family.

I recall the move in day well, it was a Saturday. There was a small factory before our section of seven houses, and a little Unity Frankfort store at the corner of 2nd and Mentor streets. An old to me, but I don't know if she was old, (German lady) Mrs. Gerger, owned, and operated this corner store. My brother Billy and I were on the front porch of our home when a boy walked past. He went in the store made a purchase and started back past us. He was eating a O'Henry candy bar, it was so tempting, I would have loved a piece of it. I called out to the boy, (*"Hey kid"*), I asked his name, he said *"Jack"*, and that he just turned four years old on his birthday September 16th. I told him, *"This is my brother Billy and he also turned four on November 5th"*. I introduced myself and stated that I was seven. I inquired with Jack, if there were any other kids in the area about my age. He told me, the boy next door to him at 213 Wyoming Avenue also named Billy **Sutton (no relation to the jail bird)** he was nine. When I met Billy, I was infatuated, at age seven, could it be love? At least that is how I felt at the time. The feelings lasted till I was almost sixteen. It was on our first, and only date, I realized we were just very good friends. Bill had his eye on the girl next door to me, Antoinette Marittizo.

I recall Bill playing his Ukulele, and he would sing a song to me. *"Five foot two Eyes of Blue, Coca, Coca, Coca, Coo, has anybody seen my gal?* I thought he just sang it to me, but I found out, he also sang it to my friend Alice Hires. (Jack) or John Joseph Rowan, as his wife Linda calls him, our first friend, is still my brother Bill's, and my best friend. All those years through thick and thin, and many moves on his part to other states, we always found each other again and again. That special Saturday, on our first day in the new home something else happened. Our kitchen sink was anchored on the inside of the old shed wall, if you can imagine, it just hung there, and we could see the very shiny gooseneck pipe just under the sink. It was so shiny. The sink was not a cabinet sink. It was just mounted like I said. Mom turned on the water to wash some dishes, suddenly there was water pouring out of the pipe flooding the kitchen floor. Well I guess back then if you purchased a home, either through the VA or FHA, there was no disclosure posted on the mortgage papers. Whoever sold this home to my parents nicely put plastic tape over a large rotted out hole in the pipe, then they took silver gloss spray paint, and sprayed the whole pipe from top to bottom. Needless to say, my parents had to wait until Monday to contact the realtor in order to have the problem rectified. Monday could not come too fast for them. On the other hand, I could have waited for a month of Monday's. Thank heavens the realtor paid the plumbing bill. My parents never had money for a rainy day, let alone a broken pipe. Monday morning, and it was time to start the march off to another new school. I thought the old school was far? I would now attend Incarnation of

Our Lord School, located at 4th and Lindley Avenue. I had to go from 2nd and Wyoming over to 3rd Street, past Louden, across Roosevelt Blvd. which was a six-lane highway, and still is; now remember when I did attempt that four-lane road at Hunting Park Ave. back when I was about four years old, but I was traveling by tricycle, now I was on my feet again. All in all, it was a nine-block walk to school one way. Why was I being persecuted like this? I hoped the next move we made would put us closer to a school and church. My next move was on me. It would not happen until I married in 1963. (Ironically) the home my husband John and I purchased in 1965 was in the same number block as the 2nd street house. Ours was 4766 Tampa St. So, I did not heed the warning to myself, about being closer to schools and church. My four sons had to walk the same distance I did, across the same six lanes at Roosevelt Boulevard, to St. Ambrose School and Church. We Py's stayed in our house on Second Street forever. Now that the walls can't talk, I will tell you about my future steps, and the rest of the ten little Py's

My new school presented a different order of Nuns; they were the Immaculate Heart of Mary Nuns. This time they were in dark blue, their hats were more rounded. I guessed they had more round faces than the other Sisters, the St. Joseph nuns seem to have square head pieces, and long faces. This was just a child's opinion. It took a while to make friends. You know I was still stuck on 28th St., and my very first school, Corpus Christi. It was very hard for me to comprehend any school work at Incarnation. I think it was because I was still traumatized. I never told anyone how I felt until I started writing this story. "The Truth Shall Set You Free" I know now, that if I could go back, and start school over. I would have whizzed through my lower grades. But we all know we can never go back. It is like when you leave toy land as a child, at Christmas, you can never cross that barrier again.

November 1949, mom, and dad had three children, I was 7 years old, brother Billy 4, and Patty 9 months, and mother was about two months in the family way. My sister Marie was due to enter this vast world by June of 1950. She was mom's smallest child; as an infant, she was very frail. Mother's baby girl got pneumonia when she was just a few months old, so much said for *infant immunity*. Our former Dr. Burrell from 33rd and Allegheny was still making house calls, but we moved too far, and he asked Mom to look for a new Dr. This is when we met Dr. Joseph Larken, by the way, at that time he and his wife had seven of their fifteen children. His office, home, and practice all in one, was located on Roosevelt Boulevard at Lawrence St., just past Fourth. It was within walking distance from our home. This was perfect since we did not own a car.

Our new doctor was not the only one that had a large family. There were other large families in our new neighborhood. The Lee family was a total of nine; they did not live far from us, seven children and the parents. I met the Small family, I think they had nine children; I went through school with Diane. I, at age seventy, am still corresponding with Mr. Walter Small her, dad. When he was in his younger years, he was a very handsome man and I can still see Mrs. Sara Small a beautiful woman. She has passed on. I think I can say Mr. Small is old by now. I hope I will live as long as he, so I can finally say I know what it is like to be old. NOTE *(Mr. Small died Nov. 16, 2015. I made the trip to St. Helena Church, in Blue Bell PA to view him and reconnect with his oldest daughter Diane.)* I remembered Mr. Small especially because he constantly practiced the Corporal Works of Mercy. When my

Father was laid out, he paid his respects. Again, nineteen years later in June of 1995 he was there for our family, as we laid our mother to rest. Some of the other big families in our parish at Incarnation of Our Lord were the Valarias, they had at least eight children, one of whom was, Barbara, and she was my age. The Shue family had seven or eight; Kathy was my Maid of Honor, when John T. Hopkins and I were married on January 5, 1963. I made a few friends who I walked to school with. My new acquaintances were, Joan O'Neill, Pat McDonald, Florence Meehan, Janette Kovalevsky, Virginia McDowell, Janette Kenna, and Agnes Callahan, and our May Procession Queen Mary Ellen O'Leary. Our home at 4722 N. 2nd Street near Wyoming Avenue was at the very end of Incarnation Parish. As I walked along, each one of the girls would fall in when I past their street or their home. All but Pat (McDonald) Butler, are still living and in good health. It must have been something in the water that keeps us going? I had one very best friend; I will refer to her as just "Jo". I am not able to get her permission to write her name. I explained to "Jo" what I was doing, by two phone calls, a few letters and two emails; to this day I have not gotten a response. I hope and pray she is well. I past her home on Memorial Day, May 27, 2013 and there were American Flags hanging outside her living room window. I mailed her a card June 5, 2013, if I remember correctly June is her birth month. I wrote a note bringing her up to date with my life. I will again send her a birthday card next week June 2014 for her 72nd birthday. She was my best friend and played a part in my youth from 2nd grade into my late teens, 18 to be exact. Today, June 8, 2014 I just mailed a letter to her sister in N.C. trying to find out if Jo is well. The letter was retuned by US Mail, stamped no one at that address. Jo's car sits outside her home all the time, I'm tempted to go knock on her door, but the unknown is better left as it is. She is just Jo as I will mention her as I continue my story.

Getting back to the beginning, by now you must have figured out that I started to adjust to this move, making new friends and this new school, even though my little legs hurt from such a long walk. I look back and think of all the extra time the girls and I had getting to know each other, and all the secrets we shared in those seven years of walking to and from school and church.

Time and years tick on, our Pie is growing larger and we are growing out of our three-bed room home. After my sister Patty, our forth sibling a girl Marie, arrived on June 12, 1950, a baby boy Joseph arrived, October 8, 1951 (mom got her Josephine in boy form) "The little King" dad called him. Today Joe and his wife Ruth are far from royalty. They are reenactors from the French & Indian War. Ruth has Indian blood? OG! I'm just kidding. This is a photo in full customs at one of their Rendezvous in Homeland, FL.

Joe & Ruth

Brother Richard, Dec.16, 1953. I often wondered about the lapse of time between my next siblings, only to find out Mom had a miscarriage. My sister Marian arrived on March 31, 1954 (The Marian Year in the Catholic Church). Kathleen was our second November baby on the 29, 1955. The youngest brother Dennis, who is my Godson, entered the PIE June 4th, 1957. It must have been like our three times Great Grandfather, Nicolas Py

Sr. who was **Godfather** for some of his older brother Jean Claude's children, or my parents just ran out of Catholics for Godparents. When Denny was born, mother informed me I would be his Godmother. If my math is correct I was 15 going on 16. God mother means if something happens to the parents, the Godparents would have to help raise the Godchild in the Catholic faith. Was I ready for that commitment? I had to obey my parents, so Godmother I am. It was during that year and a half lapse mom had another miscarriage. Finally, while I was a junior in Cardinal Dougherty High School, mother gave birth to my youngest sister Regina (Jennie) on March 30, 1959. When I think, we could have been a full dozen. Mother was in her 38th year and so was dad, they weren't getting any younger. I wonder if they just *were worn out*, or did they realize we were running out of space. Regardless, here we are the Py Clan. As my piece of pie goes on, *I will write a segment for all of my brothers, and sisters with their blessings, there is something unique to be said about each piece (person) in our pie.*

"   *When we are born, we are brought into this world by our parents, sharing their Life and their Nature.* "None of us shared the large family part of their nature. My youngest brother Dennis had six children three daughters with a first wife, and a son and two daughters with his wife Caren. Sister Kathleen and her husband Chickie had five children three girls and two boys. John Hopkins and I had four sons in four years by the time I was twenty-four, we were heading in my mother's direction. If that continued, by thirty-eight I could have been the mother of at least twelve or thirteen, O no! Brother Bill and wife Carol had four daughters, Brother Joe and Ruth had three girls and a son, Marie and her husband John had two daughters and a son, Marian and husband Chuck had two sons, and a daughter, Jeannie and husband Ed produced three sons. Patty and her first husband George had a daughter and two sons. Tom Coyle, Pat's husband is a wonderful step- father. Richard had two daughters. Altogether, Mother and Dad ended up with 36 grandchildren, 63 Great's and to date in **2015** including my seven great grandchildren, and brother Billy's great grandson Liam 6yrs. would be their two times great grandchildren. If I calculated correctly the Pie (PY FAMILY) consists of 107 of us, I may have missed one or two. I try not to make mistakes; don't hold me to the exact count. I know mom and dad are smiling. NO, they must be laughing, to be able to see what they started back in 1942. As I recall many Christmas Eve's, c. 1976 after dad passed away, all ten of us, our spouses, and our growing families (up until 1994), with a starting total fifty-five along with Mom and Uncle John, (whom had moved into the 2nd street home with her) to make fifty-seven, all of us would arrive about the same time and try to cram into that little house. Everyone would have to squish in sideways thru the living room, past mom's, very humble Christmas tree into the breakfast room, where she would have a dinner plate size, *not platters*, of cheese, pepperoni, chips, pretzels, and some holiday cookies. There would be the spiked Christmas punch, one bottle of Seagram's seven a 1/2 gallon of seven up for the adult's coke cola for the children. As holy as mom was, she could not pull off **The Loaves and Fishes.** Mother tried to have a gift card for all the grand children that included a five-dollar bill in each. Her wealth came from her yearly health insurance refund. Inevitably one or two children would get missed, what a disaster, none of us carried extra cards with us. Somehow or other we fixed mom's dilemma. Now! *Imagine* if she lived in that little house into her 90's, and we kept up that Christmas tradition, we would have to take numbers as we arrived, not to mention parking. The line to get in would have gone around the corner to Jack's old house at 211 Wyoming. What memories we have

of   211

and 4722

Each year before Christmas as we all aged, and still gather in one of our siblings, or Jack and Linda Rowans home in Narvon PA, we reminisce over our sparse, but good and happy times that we endured in the only family abode we knew, growing up in this old house at 4722 N. 2nd St.

Sometimes crying over a special memory or laughing so hard we can hardly control ourselves. Oh, and dad, dead as he is, somehow would spiritually always show his presence, like spilling a jug of wine at our camp sites or breaking the bottom out of a full punch bowl of liquored holiday cheer. It is as if he still wants to be *Home for the Holidays*. I will be bringing our holiday tales to you, as I carry my thoughts back through our Py world.

Continuing with my Step's and Schooling

I am still in the second grade and Sister, believe it or not (Incarnation) was her religious name I couldn't remember it, sorry it was still during the time of my re-adjustment. While reminiscing with Jeannette Kenna, last week 12/19/17 I was able to get Sisters name. At my age two heads are better than one. Here is my piano story. It was a Friday and the sister asked if anyone wanted to learn how to play the piano. The convent had a new nun living on campus she was musically inclined, she was not able to handle a classroom of 42 children because of a health concern, but she could teach, one on one the music chords. After school that day I left to spend my weekend at grand mom's, and Aunt Peggy was over for dinner, she and her husband Bill Bigenwald lived just around the corner on 2900 block of Taney Street. (**NOTE)** **Taney like the little league Base Ball team that made it to the play offs 2014.** Aunt Peggy worked as a secretary at Westinghouse Electric; she would come around to eat at her mom's house on the 2800 block of N. 27th Street. My Uncle John, I now realize was the bread winner, he moved the family from Chadwick Street to 27th street (it had four bedrooms), they moved in just after we moved out to our new house on Second Street. He was the one that made all the decisions. I liked their new location because I could, in the summer go back to the old swimies and try to meet up with that **old gang of mine**. It was never the same. My former friends moved on and forgot me. Anyway, I was now thinking on the lines of a new career, after being an over the road biker, a bar dancer and a runner in the pipe yard, I thought I would now try to be a concert pianist. Aunt Peggy was very interested in me and my new everything. Upon her asking me what went on in school today, I told about the piano teacher, and the cost of just $1.50 a lesson. I murmured out, "where would I get that kind of money?" My good Aunt Peggy told me to tell Sister on Monday I would be taken the lessons, she would pay for them. I must have been so excited I forgot to tell my parents of my next great adventure. I went into school and told the nun, I would be joining in with the piano class. I started the class on Tuesday, along with Treasure Solecki,

(D) 2017, Helen Mitchell, and Sandra Vacanti. I had not been told by my second-grade teacher, there would be *two lessons a week. Tuesday's and Thursday's*, and this made the cost go up to **$3.00 a week?** I also forgot to mention this little discrepancy to my aunt, let alone mom and dad. As time passed, and quite quickly, the lessons went on and my little fingers were learning how to play the piano. One day the piano Sister asked when she could expect to be paid for her talents. I told her how *my Aunt Peggy was going to be paying for the lessons*. The nun gave me a note for mom and dad and enclosed a big bill of $36.00 for the past six weeks of lessons. Back then this lump sum of cash was what a food budget for a week would be. Mom and dad were speechless to say the least. Where were they to get this amount of cash to pay the dear Sister? *"Who told you to join the class?"* (As before, when Aunt Margret had asked how I got to her home, when I was just a little girl on my trike). I innocently look them in the eye and told the truth; *"Aunt Peggy was going to pay for my lessons" she told me so*, **NOT?** As I specified in the beginning of this tale, no one ever told us anything about anyone or things that were going on in our family. Everything was on a need to know basis. It was then I found out, Aunt Peggy was going to have her first child, (Bill Jr.) and because of her frail condition, she would have to stop working. Uncle Bill and she would now be on a planned budget. Aunt Peggy would not be able to pay for any past or future lessons. I immediately learned how to **budget**. Not money, but time. I found myself after school and at recess, working off my debt, in the convent. When my obligation was satisfied, the nun told me I could take singing lessons for just 25 cents a week. Before I ventured into this singing career, I got permission from my parents to spend a quarter, *to better my vocal cords*. I never made it past the alto section of the choir; well what did I expect for two bits a week, miracles? By May of 1950, the Incarnation Glee club, were able to sing a song in English at our First Communion Ceremony, I was part of that gleeful group of all girls. I forgot to tell how Aunt Peggy and her friend Mary Jennings met my great grandfather the firefighter. I was an infant, they were my baby sitters on one Sat. night. The two girls, not one went down stairs from the Apt. to get a Coke Cola next door at the candy store. The Apt. door locked in back of them, what to do? over to the fire house for help. My great grandfather introduced himself to them, and **who** he was. He save me and the two of them. What a revolting predicament teenagers can get into without trying; their innocence alone kept them out of trouble.

I found third and fourth grades not very eventful. Only two visions come to mind as far as third grade. Our class room was located in an attic above the lunch room, and auditorium, the stationary closet for the whole school was up there also, just off from our classroom, and this closet did not have full flooring, just rafters. Sister went into the closet to fill an order of supplies for one of the other grades. While we and the boy that came to pick up the supplies waited and waited, Sister did not come out. The lunch time bell rang, and no one moved from their desk, but I did, I walked over opened the door, and there was Sister, all I could see was the top part of her torso. Sister's two legs were through the floor and hanging down into the lunch room. After what seemed like an hour, only minutes, another nun walking through the auditorium, must likely looking up and praying to God, happened to see legs hanging from the ceiling, and came to Sister's aid. She was not hurt but very embarrassed. The second occurrence, I distinctly remember, in the third grade in the early 50's, all the children who attended Catholic Schools were administered the sacrament of Confirmation by the Bishop of the Archdiocese. (Now days it is seventh grade, and more understandable). Well we had to take a second name, (one of a Saint). It was about two weeks before we were to be Confirmed, sister told us she needed our new name printed on the form she handed to each of us. We were to bring it back when we returned to school after lunch. I hurried home, told mom I needed my saint's name written on the form, and sister wanted it today. Well if you can imagine the chaos that took place back then in our house at lunch, and any time; you must guess, I left without my name on the paper. I wanted to use the saint's name of the church I was baptized in, Saint **Bridget**. Of course, I could not remember her name only that it started with a **B**. Here I am back from lunch and no name on the blank piece of paper. Sister walk up and down the aisles of all our desks and took each girl slip, with pride, she would read aloud the name everyone had picked and make a pleasing comment. By the time she reached my seat, I was in a panic. *"Miss Py, where is your slip?"* (*I wanted to say under my uniform*? *"You know the one with your saint's name* on it." All I could do was look up at that very stern face and wish myself off this earth. *"Well what name did you have in mind since it is not in writing?"* I always tried to tell the absolute truth, even when threatened. *"Sister"*, I said*," I want to take the saints name of the church I was baptized in."* *"OK", she said, "I will put it on the form for you, what is her name my dear"?* *"I only know it starts with a B"*, I answered in a very low whisper, *"a B"* she echoed back to me. *"This presents a problem my dear",* Yes? I shook my head in a yes manner. I was unable to speak, which was and is **very** unusual for me. *"Well, what will it be?"* She started the litany of all the woman saints that began with the letter *"B"* I was so confused, and afraid, by the time she got to Saint Bernadette, I blurted out, *"that's it".* *"Well this is a beautiful name"* the nun commented, she proceeded to tell me, *"The Blessed Mother appeared to her at Lourdes," "Is that why you picked her name"?* My problem was, it is not the one I wanted, but I was scared straight, if you can put yourself in my place at nine years old. I shook my head again in a yes mood, *as not to tell a lie*. This is how I became Elaine Bernadette Py. One of the problems was, it was too long, and I could not spell that name. I should have said Mary, but being as truthfully as I could, I am who I am. I do carry Bernadette as part of my full name to this day and She has stuck by me since the third grade. Something else happened while we were receiving **The Holy Spirit**. Beside the light slap on the cheek by the worthy Bishop, we as a group had to raise our right hand and take a pledge of *temperance*. We promised him, we would not drink any alcoholic beverages until we reach the ripe age of 21. Gee, I thought to myself, I will be old at 21. That was and still is the legal age for one to be able to drink. If we broke this agreement, we should expect a visit from the **Paraclete** *himself*, and who really knew what would happen to anyone that did not hold to this very important vow. I held true to the contract, and on my 21st birthday at Palumbo's Restaurant and Night Club, I had my first alcoholic beverage. It was a frozen whiskey sour, it was an excellent recommendation and I enjoyed my first alcoholic beverage, and well worth waiting for. Although, as I sipped my drink, I keep looking around to see if there was a **white dove** anywhere in the building. You do know, South Philadelphia is noted for doves flying freely all around. I was safe and protected by the **Holy Spirit**. People to this day laugh at me for keeping that very important pledge. Note: No matter how I felt about the way some of the Sisters treated me, it was just my feelings. All the nuns gave their lives to God, and they had to put up with a lot of stubborn, spoiled children. But I was neither of the above. I loved the good Sisters.

Incidentally by fourth Grade, a pair of round wire  rimed eye glasses now accompanied the bridge of my nose. I had been taken to the school nurse, along with the rest of the class, in groups of eight. I had to read the eye chart; this was unwelcome news, because I could only see the top two largest lines, forget the rest. I guessed at it, and completely failed the eye exam test, that was no surprise to me I failed almost all my scholastic tests. Money was scarce at home, with food bills, and maternity ward cost. I had to go to a free clinic for the glasses I needed. They were to better my sight, but oh did I look horrible. I will tell you, I did not need this added attraction. Everyone called me four eyes. Well now, I had a choice, I could be *PIE FACE*, or *FOUR EYES*, big deal I just wanted to be me. (See Ed Wynn's photo in this story, pg. 118.

Fifth Grade had to be one of my worse years. I do remember the nun in charge of that class. It was Sister Costello. She looked old; she was short and very round. I was having a terrible time comprehending my school work. I think because I did not cause any trouble in school, (I was a good girl) all the nuns just mainstreamed me right on to high school. While keeping Sister Costello company at age ten, this one day, sometime after Christmas we had to ware regular street clothes to school. Our uniforms were to be sent to the **dry cleaners**, so they would look presentable for some special occasion coming up. My uniform was cleaned at home with ammonia and hung out on the back line to dry. It had a strong smell that ammonia. On the so-called dress down day, I entered the class room in a dark blue skirt with a white blouse; I wore a blue pleated neck scarf around my neck, with a pendent of my initial **E** hanging from it. This was the newest styles that year; my Aunt Dot gave it to me for Christmas. I walked pass the nun to get to my seat. She called out to me, "*Miss Py, how dare you wear an E for effort in this class room.*" "*Go stand in the corner for the day*". If I spent the day facing the wall, how would I ever get the will to ascertain a subject she was trying to teach the class? I will never forget that woman, or her name. We children endured a lot from different nuns through our years in school. On behalf of Sister Costello, it has come to my attention, that if I had spent more time in a library, rather than just sitting on the front steps of the only two I knew. One was on 5th Street near Tabor Road, and the other on Wyoming Ave. near C St. Maybe I could have worn that "**E**" for effort, rather than just using it as my initial medallion. During this time, as I write in my later years, just living down the street from the East Cheltenham Community Library, I have visited this vast hall of information, where the knowledge in the books, and DVD's can take you into a whole new world of education, travel, and fantasy. When I was young, I just went into a library when I needed to do a report. My motto was, get in and out as fast. The book shelves in the library that were filled with words frightened me, because I was not a proficient reader, and my comprehension was poor. In the 1940's, 50's and 60's CORA did not exist in the Catholic School system. There were no special education programs, or one on one help for someone as myself. If only I had known? What a fool, not to have taken advantage of the wealth of information stored in the library. In using it, I may have set myself on a straight course to a better education. I now know, it is never too late to improve your brain. I just finished reading an article written by **Nancy Post**, a resident at PPH. (Philadelphia Protestant Home in the Lawndale section of Philadelphia), where I have joined their fitness center. I must share her article with you. She writes: **All About Libraries ..." *Reading? Nice? It's the thing," said the Library Mouse solemnly as he leaned forward. "Believe me, my young friend, there is nothing-absolutely nothing-half so much worth doing as simply messing about with books. Simply messing," he went on dreamily; "messing-about. "Mouse went on composedly, looking up with a pleasant laugh, hard cover or not , it doesn't matter, that's the charm of it. Whether you get transported away, or whether you never get anywhere at all, your always engaged. if you get carried away to a new destination or you just reach a familiar place. The mouse states no matter what you read you are always engaged.(I cut it short). He the mouse invites us to go to the library and make a day of it." Ms. Post states this is adapted from, "The Wind in the Willows," by Kenneth Grahame.* I wish I had met these two writers when I was a young girl, and open minded for help, I would have been carried off to the wonderful world of fantasies, historical facts and that geography I did not think I needed.

On the lighter side of being in fifth grade, or ten years of age, girls could join the Girl Scouts of America. I joined with a few other girls. I mentioned some of them earlier, Treasure (D 2016) Sandra, the two Virginia's, and a few others. We were off on a new adventure. The troop was #620; we met in Incarnation's school hall every Friday evening from seven to nine PM. A single lady (Dottie Navel), Mrs. Devlin, and Mrs. Baker were the troop leaders. Joining girl scouts was one of the most important decisions I was able to make in my young life. I stayed in Scouts all the way through my senior year of high school. I wished I could have continued to become a Girl Scout Leader. Unfortunately, I had to work on Friday nights to help our financial situation at home. To this day, c.2014-15) I tell my granddaughters, Brigid age fourteen, Moira ten, and Sinead eight all about my scouting days, and the fun I had camping one weekend a month. It's funny how memories recall separate occasions in one's life. I am reflecting on a revolting development that happened to me on my very first camping trip. I just turned ten, it was a chilly

September and our first camping trip was to a primitive area in Coatesville, PA The camp was called Silver Springs; it sported a log cabin with a wood fire place in it. We had canvas army cots for beds (hard as a rock), and I thought my bed at home was hard. Most of my friends had new quilted down sleeping bags, but Dad got me one from the Army & Navy Store, it was an army surplus bag made with an itchy army blanket. I just had to make do. The cabin did not have a toilet, Hmm! How strange I thought. We were directed down a dark path and showed a little rectangular type house, Miss Navel called it "Johnny on the Spot" (outhouse), I never heard of such a place. She explained it was our toilet. Oh my, I thought to myself, how do I flush it? Of course, I found out fast it did not have a flusher. We were told if we had to go during the late night, we were to use a galvanized wash bucket out on the front porch. She did not mention it was only for liquid use. I am an innocent girl and having to use the bucket during the wee hours of the AM., I quietly got out of my itchy cold cot, and went out to the freezing cold bucket and deposited a big one. Daylight could not come fast enough for me; I knew the sun would warm me up. As I stretched to get out of bed, Miss

Navel enter the cabin and stated, *"Who did it?"* I continued to dress. She again repeated her question in a much louder stern voice, it caught my attention. It was then I realized, it was I Who did it. I fess up, and I had to take the full bucket from all the girls (wees) down to see Johnny and deposit its contents without a spill. After I completely scoured the darn bucket, it was only then. I realized it was not for a BM, in the PM. When I told my granddaughters this story they got a big chuckle over Grum's BIG mistake. I also elaborated to them about a two-week trip by rail out to **Pikes Peak, Colorado Springs, CO.** in 1959. It was a scouting Jamboree for 3,500 girls from all over the world. The younger two girls do not know about the man in the Pullman car next to our train, (see pg.165) but I did tell the oldest, she laughed and said she could not wait to go for a train ride like the one I was on. Brigid now a senior, Moira a junior, and Sinead a brownie is in the scouting program, but the only thing that has not changed is the Girl Scout cookie sales. Oh yes, the price of a box of cookies has changed immensely, they were only fifty cents when I sold them door to door. Today in the Montgomery County Council the price is now $4.00 a box. I will take the olden days over this prohibitive cost, fast paced world.

My memory drew a blank about anything in sixth grade until I ran into Beverly Young at a Memorial Day Service, she reminded me she transferred into Inky at 6th, we talked about Sister St. Henry the nun who tried to help me with my marks, that were just passing as usual. I would stay up to about 10:00 PM each night, with mom next to me at our kitchen table; she was trying to help me get the home work into my blocked head. I do recall this one evening, it was late, and we were both tired. Our eat-in kitchen door led out to the old shed, where the ice box was stored in earlier years. Our refrigerator was now located in our interior kitchen. The shed was old and full of stuff. Brooms, mops, and buckets have taken refuge out there. Now suddenly, a loud noise from that dark room blared into our space. *"Mom was the outside door locked today?"* I whispered, mother had a blank look on her face, I was afraid, so was she, I never saw her like this. Dad was in bed as the rest of the clan was. We both quietly, and quickly got up from the table, I put my books away, and mother crept over to the inter door, and slid the dead bolt over, we put out the light, and I can't remember who got up the stairs first, or if we were side by side, we made it to the top floor, I went directly to bed and mother to her room. I had no problem getting to sleep, it seems like I just shut my eyes, and she was calling dad and the rest of us to get up for work and school.   It was winter, the ancient heater was churning the steam heat through the old iron radiators, and steam pipes. I could smell the coffee, hot chocolate, and oatmeal aroma coming up the same steps we ran up only hours ago. When I reached the bright of day, and the light of the kitchen, I hesitated for a moment, and then asked mom, if she had opened the door to the shed yet? *"Yes"*. she echoed from the refrigerator door. *"Well"*? With a question in my voice, dad and my siblings were all ears by then. No one was interested in the wonderful breakfast mother had prepared. Everyone wanted to know our dilemma. Mom opened the door between the two rooms, and across the door frame was a mop with the bucket on top of it, the younger boys Joe five, and Richie four years old got out in the shed, while she was hanging wash in the yard the day before, Joe and Richie were playing Knights in Shining Armor. Mom said, *"One of the Knights must have collapsed while on duty and fell against the kitchen door last night."*   *"He certainly shrugged his duty of protecting us"* I said. No one understood, because mom and I did not give up that we were frightened by the noise. Everyone sat down to breakfast and the school day began without a hitch. Later that afternoon mom and I had a hearty laugh.

When I was in seventh grade, a substitute lady teacher replaced Sister Helena an older nun, who had been sick for about a month or two. Funny while the sub was teaching, I was starting to comprehend most of the work, but not the diagramming of a sentence, or geography, I could not for the life of me understand, how this stuff would be of any help to me in a family setting, so there it was, another mental block. If I had taken advantage of the Free Library System, I would have discovered a world of resourceful information. **Note**: to people like myself, it's never too late to go to a library. In this quite place, if you open your ears, you will hear the books calling out to you. I did. When the nun recouped from whatever her aliment was, and she was back to school, I was back to not learning again. One day she gave out blank paper for us to take a book test or something? She had to leave the classroom for a little while which was very often. I made a mistake on the page, and my eraser made even more of a mess. Mary Ellen Kane was left in charge of our class when Sister would have to leave the room. I told Mary Ellen I needed to go to the closet for a clean sheet of paper, she said *OK*. Off I went, upon returning to my desk, Sister walked in the room. She started right at me. *Talk about the flying nun. This woman was faster than a speeding bullet.* As she landed in front of my desk, I knew I was doomed. *Why, Dear Lord, is this happening to me?* There she was standing over me, "*why are you prancing around the room **Miss Py**?*" I tried to explain! I stated earlier on, I really think some of the nuns I encountered **did not have** *ears*. Sister Helena never heard a word I said. She escorted me out of the room, past Mother Superior's office and into the back of our auditorium. I got a scolding, and she shook me at the shoulders, then sent me back to the classroom. As I passed the Superior's office, Francis O'R..., a gofer, and informant for the nuns, was lurking about outside the office, when I walked past him, I had a smile on my face. He didn't know it, **but I was smiling at him**. I entered the class room and went right to my seat. I picked up my pencil and continued to try to catch up on the test. Suddenly, ***there she was standing over me again***.

This time she had me by the back of my neck, "*come with me*" it was deja 'vue, I just got back from a trip with the flying nun. Where were we off to now and why? I went right along, I had no choice I was in her grip, as she passed the blackboard she grabbed her yard stick. What was this all about? I wondered. We were right back where we were a few minutes before. "*You'll laugh at me will you*" she said, with a very stern voice. I did not say one word. Then she whacked me across the back of my legs with the yard stick and whacked me again. "*Now get back to class*" she screamed. I took the same route as before, passing no other than Francis outside the Superior's office. I was not smiling on this trip. There he was proud as a peacock. It was then I realized he told the nun I had a smile on my face upon returning from the first encounter. What a snitch. I often wondered what became of him. I am most positive of this, I ran into a cousin of his about six years ago, Father, Steve Kats ... and if I am not mistaken Francis title is no other than Father Francis O'R... of the Harrisburg, PA, Diocese. I must laugh now and wonder if he ever thought back to his snitching days and is that a matter for confession. I never told my mom or dad of the whacking, I was afraid, that just on principle I would get another one. I know the old saying, "Three's a Charm", but this charm was not one I wanted added to my collections of spankings. In my heart, and mind, I did not deserve any of what some of the nuns dished out.

At last I made it to eight grade, we were finally the upper classmen. Most of my girlfriends by sixth and seventh grades had boyfriends from our school. When they walk to school all the couples would hold hands or fool around teasingly. My friend "Jo" and I started to go to school a little earlier, as not to interfere with the ones that had stars in their eyes. I must admit, we and a few others were considered the wall flowers. Looking back, yes, I know for a fact. I was. The girls with steady beau's didn't bother with us girls that weren't lucky enough to land a fellow. They were always with the boys. Than too: beauty was in the eyes of the beholder. I was a late bloomer. Inky held dances for the seventh and eighth grades, me and my friends without boyfriends would go, hoping to get asked to dance. We never did get to a slow dance; my friends that paired off were the only ones to glide through waltzing in each other's arms. Jo and I would wait to be asked to dance by some of the boys that were not in the so call

"Click"' they stood over on the opposite side of the hall and just hung around talking, and finally that **Good** Night *Sweet Hear*t song would start playing, the dance would be over. We would leave and say maybe the next dance would be our chance. The fall of 1955 to the spring of 1956 school year went so fast, we had a Spring Minstrel Show with black face and all, the whole school participated. Dad helped Bill's fifth grade class with a String Band theme, and grand mom Weldon made the costumes for all forty-two boys. We 8th grade girls had Joan O'Neil sing and Janet Kovolesky did a ballet. The girls from my old piano class took turns playing tunes during the show. The production was a smash. We have the nuns and parents to thank for this hit. To my knowledge they never had another show.

Graduation was a few weeks away. Our whole class had to wear the same fancy powder blue gown made by a dress company, picked by the nuns, this was not a clever idea for anyone without a perfect figure, liked eight grade girls really had figures, I guess some did, but I did not have one. Well you know what I mean. I was one of the not so nicely shaped people. To look half decent in this

Mary Like dress, I needed a bra to hold me up and in place. I was about the ripe size of between a 36-38 C in the bosom area. Mother being very small, measured in at a 34 B size. Why am I telling this to

everyone? Well, with the price of the dress, shoes, gauntlets, (by the way I had beautiful gauntlets made for my second wedding), Oh and a wreath for my head, & the cost of the photo, my parents ran out of cash. Mom gave me one of her only three bras to put on, as an under garment, what a disaster, like a *pea nut on a pumpkin*, I was pulled and pushed into mother's brassiere. Here I was on the brink of a young adolescent, and still had no say. It didn't matter much, as it turned out graduation week was just approaching, and our house was under quarantine, almost all of us came down with Scarlet Fever, or maybe Scarlet Tina, regardless no one could leave or come into our abode until the incubation period was up. The health department plastered a big yellow sign on our front and back doors. (**House under Quarantine**) I guess that sign was better than the one I saw on our first home in 1949 **(Foreclosure)**, I barely made all the various school activities set for graduation, in the end all turned out fine.

Now don't we all look marvelous, in our identical blue dresses, with our May Queen Mary Ellen O'Leary, and Bishop Cletus J. Benjamin? God bless his young soul. You know back in those days when mom was young, all the woman wore girdles. Not because they were fat, it gave them better posture. Our mom was a petite person; she was 92 lbs. on her wedding day and 128 when she died. She did not need a girdle, on the other hand, I could have used one at the time, but I would have never looked like an hour glass shape girly. I will tell you more about mom's yearly girdles later, they are a funny part of her, and as time goes by they come into play, or should I say (**PLAYTEX**)? Mom wore that type of girdle; I will tell you stories about her, and her wealthy garment, later in this tale. I will be entering Cardinal Dougherty High School, in September of 1956. I will write about this beautiful new school, and my adventures in time,

as I

journey through my memoirs.

In June 1956 we had an eight-grade graduation party at our house, and I received some

gifts of cash, and one special gift from my Uncle John Weldon. He was my Godfather; he had given me a nice watch with a brown leather band on it as a graduation gift. I was grateful, but it was not very girlish. **The Bulova Watch story comes when I tell of my brother Dennis.** Uncle John was a single man, (he is shown in his US Army uniform on pg. 102,) so he didn't know what girls liked, but he did take the full responsibility of the job of a God Father, he and a gift was always there for my birthdays, graduations, my wedding, and the births of my four sons. In this fast pace, electronically controlled twenty-first century it would be almost impossible to find another John J. Weldon. He was the sole provider for his mother's family (Grand mom). He enlisted in the US Army in 1943. As a young soldier he said goodbye to the girl he was to marry, and all his family members, he was sent to France and the Philippine Theater in the Second World War. My Uncle John could not write home much while over in the war, but mom, his other sisters and grand would correspond as often as possible to keep his spirits up. He received only one letter from his girl, it started "*Dear John*", but it was a real "*Dear John*" letter and the ring was with it. My Uncle kept that ring forever, and never bothered with any other girls. He continued, after the war to take care of his mother, and his younger siblings. That was Uncle John, **and take note**, Uncle John Weldon was the last person my dear first husband John T. Hopkins saw, before his own death that took him home to the Lord on **November 30, 1999**. Note: Uncle John had already passed away on **June 28, 1999**. I often wonder about that visit from my deceased uncle. My husband told me he saw my uncle at our basement door on Tuesday the week before he himself died. He double checked to make sure he was not seeing things. No, my uncle was in our home. When my John asked my uncle what he was doing here, Uncle said "Checking things out, just checking things." This was how my uncle talked. They say, "The last to die come back in some form to see you before you die." I guess it is true?

I am reflecting over years passed since my grade school days, it is now February 15, 2014, and as I sit here on the lanai outside our condo overlooking the Myakka River, in Port Charlotte, FL., which is situated on the Gulf Coast, the geography subject comes to my mind. After celebrating my twelfth wedding anniversary (D of M February 14,

2003) with my second husband also named (John), last evening we enjoyed Valentine's at the swanky Hills Restaurant, in the Rotunda West Golf & Country Club in Florida. As a young girl, places like this did not exist. So many memories of my youth flash before me. I revealed before, Geography did not interest me, so I would never in my wildest dream, have thought of spending winters in such a warm and lovely place, but here I am for the seventh consecutive year enjoying one of the most magnificent views.; where Palm trees, Pelicans, Dolphins, and even Tree Frogs that come right up to our window, to feed on the bugs, attracted by our inside lights, nature, flowing rivers, canals, and Crane Birds were so far out of my reach in my youth as a Py girl growing up. All of this could only be a dream. I do believe dreams can come true; and the geography I ignored, would have clued me in on all

God's glory and such beauty. John and I will start north about end of March, but we have all our future winters to look forward to. Spring and, summer in Cheltenham, PA is always full of enchanting adventures. As you read, you can see I am resigning myself to the start of getting **just a little old**. I have approached my peak in life and will be heading down **these steps** on this easy path. I have a long way to go, and a lot more to contribute regarding my life in our Py home. I jumped ahead again, so I will bring you back to the "Pie" as it grew and some interesting fillings.

A Big Break for Dad - New Job   C.1951

Dad would take the public transportation to Midvale Steel where he was employed as a welder. While he waited at the top of our corner to get the trolley, his eyes would wander down Wyoming Ave. just over the railroad bridge, to a large one-story brick building. He would walk past this property from time to time; on the way to Goldenberg's Candy Factory or further on to the German bakery. The name on that building was *Carrier Air Conditioning Corporation.* One very hot summer day, he decided to stop in, and see if he could purchase a window air conditioning unit for our home, direct from the manufacturer. Our home never had an air conditioner. We were lucky if we had screens or a swivel fan. Dad entered the building by a side door that happened to be open at lunch time. He was approached by one of the employees who inquired, if he could help with my father's needs. When dad asked about buying a unit, it was then he found out the inter components were not made at this facility. This was a sheet metal shop that did the casings for the units. Basically, all the welding was done in that branch. Dad expressed to the man he was a welder and asked if the company was hiring. The gentlemen called for a supervisor to come over, *"hey this fellow says he can weld."* The supervisor gave my father a protective welder's shield to put on, and handed him a torch, Dad was directed to weld a seam on one of the casing boxes. Dad took the torch and followed the directions. When he was finished the weld, to the surprise of the foreman and the doubting watchers, the seam was invisible. The bead as it was called was clean, and clear. Dad was told **Carrier** was a union shop, and they would hire him on the spot, however he would have to join Local 19, the Sheet Metal Workers Union, and the entrance fee to join was a mere $119.00. Where on this earth were my parents to get that kind of cash? The pay scale dad would receive for eight hours work, would outweigh the fee, if he had that kind of cash. Mom and dad were just getting back on their feet & a new baby on the way. This amount of money was a dream. Well, the dream came true. I do not know where or how they conjured up the $119.00, but they did, and dad was hired by **Carrier Air Condition Cor.**. In the mid 1950's dad hourly salary was $5.55 an hour. It was like moving on to easy street, and dad only had to cross the street, turn the corner and he was in work. Times were good for a long while, but all good things eventually end. During his tenure at Carrier, he and his co-workers had habits, some were gambling, and Py liked to play cards. The card games were for real cash, (no IOU's) and most of the men thought they could double their bucks, dad was one of them. Some of the other habits were their beers. So, if the guys weren't gambling in the back of the shop on pay day, they would head down the corner to the Feltonville Inn, and have a few. Monday to Thursday dad would be home by 5:05 PM for our dinner, which was on the table between 5:15 & 5:30 PM but, we never knew what time to expect him home on a Friday night. Most of the Friday nights mom would serve us children our usual no meat Friday night dinner by 5 PM or so. Baked macaroni, potato pancakes, or scrambled eggs. If the cards were in dad's favor, he would arrive about 6:30 or 6:45 with his full pay and some extra cash. On those nights' dad would have a wind fall of money, I would be sent to the oyster house to get an oyster stew or, up to the Chinese take-out for Shrimp Chow Mein. These were luxuries we children were not privy to while at an early age. Most likely we would not like it anyway. On some occasions, Mom and Dad would have me keep an eye on my younger siblings, after they were put to bed, then my parents would gussie up and go down to the Feltonville Inn for a night cap. The Inn is where they met Jack and Pearl Kenny. This childless couple, a few years senior to my parents lived just around the corner, on Mentor Street. Jack was an over the road truck driver, and Pearl was *("just his PEARL".)* She simply stayed at home and looked as beautiful as her name. At that time is when our parents became good friends with this very generous couple. On nights when the Kenney's we're not at the Inn, mom and dad would go around to their home to socialize. Jack owned a very nice automobile, and his Pearl did not drive. The Py's, on the other hand, or should I say foot, did not have a car and dad did drive, we had our God given feet. When Jack would go on the road, he would be gone for two or more weeks at a time. Pearl needed to be driven to the beauty shop, the PA State Store (now called Wine and Spirit's) the food store etc. Jack gave dad the extra set of keys to his **automobile** and told my father, if he would take Pearl to do her errands, dad could use the car for our family, so we sort of had a car from time to time. Taking all this into account, I called dad's gig, ***Driving Miss Pearl***. Everyone benefited from this good deed. Some Friday nights when Jack would invite my parents around their house, Jack would order Tomato Pies from Charlie's Pizzeria it was Jacks treat. The leftovers were sent home with my mom, that was when I was introduced to Pizza Pie or Tomato Pie, I was about twelve. A lot of children in today's time gets pizza as soon as they have teeth and can hold a slice.   Now all was not ideal for dad or was it mom, with the driving arrangement   because, dad being an only child, and surrounded by all us kids, he would stay for **a** beer or more, after the errands were done, **just to unwind?** Dad would forget to come home as usual.

In due time mom would send Billy, and I to fetch him. I must mention, Pearl and Jack had a basement refrigerator full of beer, and all flavors of **soda** not only that, a **Charlie Chip** man delivered fresh chips and pretzels every week to the Mentor Street property. My brother and I would arrive at the door, and Pearl would say "come in, help yourselves to a soda, I will bring out the chips." For me that was like going back in time, when I was an only child, who was sent to the taproom to fetch my father. Dad and I never went straight home. My brother and I would also forget to tell dad, that we were sent to bring him home. Eventually, mother herself would arrive, she **tried** to keep her cool, but I could see the steam coming through., and I don't mean from an oven This sort of thing would go on as long as the Kenny's lived on Mentor Street. It was difficult for my father to have friends that wanted for nothing, when he had to bring every dollar home to meet all the expense that came with our large growing Py family.

OUR-SHOES

Everyone in the family had their turn for new shoes, it came on a need basis. If you had holes in your soles, and the cardboard from the cereal box was more than the leather on the bottom of the shoe, than it was your turn to get a well needed new pair of shoes. I walked to school many of days in the rain, with a hole and cardboard in my shoe, and if the school children had to go to mass, and kneel at the altar, to receive Communion; I would cross my feet as I knelt, and hope the best foot was showing. *I was taught to always put my best foot forward.* With the recent changes in the church rules, we now stand to receive our Lord. When I would stay at grandmoms on weekends, Aunt Dot would take me to the Shoe Bootery located at 22nd and Dauphin streets. If she got a bargain, she would purchase a pair for me, after she picked out her newest style. While she was being fitted, I would go over to this machine. I would climb up on it putt my feet under the viewer, I could see my feet and all the bones in my foot. It was like an X-Ray. I like looking at my bony feet. One time, the proprietor told me I had nice feet for a little girl, I blurted out that my Dad told me, I had **Polack feet**. Not knowing the nationality of this person, (Polish) of course, I laughed as I continued to chatter on. Naturally the proprietor was offended by me making fun of the Polack's. My aunt was mortified, she did a soft shoe type statement, apology, and we left the store with two pair of shoes. I was scolded for hurting his feelings. I ran back into the Bootery, and told him, I was sorry. He shook my small hand. This tale ended on the good foot. But not all the shoes stories did.

Back to dad and his antics. There was this one time the boys, Joseph, and Richard; ages seven and eight both needed shoes at the same time. We always went back down to 28th and Allegany Ave. to Dick Crain Department Store for our clothing, shoes, and other household items; I think dad got a discount because of being in the old string band. Mom handled all the financial dealings, and any money dad brought home as a pay. Mother gave dad enough cash for the two pair of shoes, and carfare for the bus. It was a Saturday, and the three of them set out on the shoe journey. They would walk up to 5th St to catch whatever PTC vehicle would arrive first, (47, 50 trolleys or the R bus, at the Blvd.) Naturally dad couldn't pass a taproom without stopping in to rest his feet? It was the magnetism of the 4/40 bar just off the corner of 5th and Wyoming that captured him in for a cold one, before heading to the bus. He got the boys a soda, and a beer for himself, time ticked by, beer after beer went down, the next thing he knew, so did the cash. WHAT TO DO? Not enough for two pair of shoes and bus fare. Dad walked the two boys down 5th street to Hunting Park Avenue and over to Second St. to the Hunting Park Bowling Lanes, went in paid the pin boy behind the counter $2.00 rent for two pair of shoes in my two brother's sizes. Joe was size nine and Rich an eight, so naturally the shoes had a 9 and or an 8 on the back of each shoe, and the colors were red and tan or green and tan. When the boys and dad arrived home with the rented shoes, my mother didn't know whether to cry, scream, or laugh. My brothers had to wear those rented shoes for two weeks every day to school, until the next pay period came around. I don't know if the shoes were ever returned to the bowling alley. This was just one of dad's many capers. He had a whole life time of them, **as I tell on my dad**.

Mom had told me about a time, before I was born; dad had come home from US Army boot training, just before being shipped over to the War. Dad, and she were out on the town, and he sure liked his beer. Dad had a little too much to drink, maybe more than he could handle. When they got home dad was very sick, (Nauseated). Oh, I forgot to tell you he had upper false teeth, why at such an early age I never asked. Well after being so sick from the night before, and in a rush to catch the Army bus, he arrived at the staging point without his teeth. An Army Sergeant yelled "Private PY, where are your teeth?" Dad didn't even know they weren't in in mouth. Mom found them clinging to the box spring under their bed, she shipped them to him. This story was given to me when I was much older. It was about the only thing mom ever told me about my father and his past.

HAIR! BAD HAIR, GOOD HAIR, NO HAIR

I had a few of my own capers as a youngster and being the oldest, I had to watch some of the younger children while mom tended to the chores of the home. Now when their little king Joe was two, he had rings of curls all over his blond head. I would take him out to the playground and other places. Everyone I would meet would say, "What is your sister's name?" My comment was always the same, "his name is Joseph, and he is my brother". *"Oh Yeah right".* I would almost have to prove he was a boy some of the time. Being a *RED HEAD*, my impatience with this ongoing type conversation got the best of me, *I had it.* I went to the barber shop down Wyoming Ave, and told Jack the barber, "If you give my baby brother a boy haircut, I will do work around the shop, sweep the floor, or any little job to pay for the cut". *"What will you Mother say when she sees the boy"? "I don't care; I'm the one that gets all the ribbing".* Jack cut Joe's curly hair and gave me a lock of curls in a brown bag, to take home to mom. I entered our home, and mom said, *"Where's little Joey?" "On the porch,"* I stated,

"Well bring him in", mom said, *"Mother I have to show you something first"*. I handed her the bag with the hair in it. She looked very angry at first, but when she saw her new little boy, she just smiled. **Boy!** Not **Girl** anymore. Boy was I lucky that time.

All ten of us Py children have beautiful hair we acquired from both our parents. By the time I was in third grade, my not so curly red hair was so long, it was way past my shoulders to my angelic wings. Mother would take the time to make two nice long braids. I always looked neat going to school. It was no fun standing while she would start the braid process. I remember well, a sip of the morning coffee, a puff of the cigarette, back to pulling the three parts of each side into the braids. Back, and forth, hair, coffee, and a puff, finely I was done, and on my way. Now at night, taking out the plait' s and all the knots, that had to be combed or briskly brushed out, was more painful than the pulling in the morning. I would scream, move out of the way so she could not brush the hair. This was a daily and evening ritual. One Saturday mother and I went for a walk, *"Mom where are we going?"* I asked. *"We are heading to the hair dressers."* I was told, *"Oh! are you getting a new doo"*? I asked. *"NO, you are"* she said." *OH"*! When the woman who cut my long beautiful red hair got done, and gave me a Tony Perm, I kid you not, I was the spitting image of ED Wynn. He was a popular American comedian, and actor noted for his **Perfect Fool** comedy character. For me to say I looked like him was not a compliment. If some of you don't know who he was or what he looked like, I have tried to give you a visual and I did locate this photo of him. He was a comic, so he had to look the part. He had a curly clump of hair on the top of his head; he covered it with a much too small hat that would blow off if a gust of wind came. More curly clumps of hair coming out of each side of his head, around his ears, which made the hat look strange. Mr. Wynn wore round wire   rimmed   glasses it suited his character, but for me, I looked horrible, and in fourth grade when I got the same type glasses, I could have just crawled under a pool table to hide. Ed was noted to have done the same in one of his skits.   I   was   not   trying   out   for   a job as a comedian, but I could have passed for his kid.

My sisters Patty and Marie were called "Irish Twins", they were just a year and three months apart. Mother dressed them alike when she could, and grand mom would make identical sets of clothing for them. Patty

had dark blondish hair and Marie had brown. They did not look alike. To make things easy, mom made sure their hair was cut very short, photo taken before the haircuts, but if you ask the girls now, they will tell you they looked like little Dutch Boys, better yet; it looked as though someone put a bowl on their heads and cut around it. Boy the growing pains were rough for me and my siblings.

Then there were the **cooties**. At one time or another everyone got them, it was a school thing. You caught them in school and brought them home to everyone in the house. People called it an *epidemic*. If you caught them your parent would send *you* to the drug store to get the medication to cure the **BUG,** the victim would have to have this medicated stuff called (Benzyl-T) put on the head, wrap the head in a towel let the stuff burn your scalp and then have it wash out. A nit comb would be used to get everything out. I was lucky in grade school, I never got them. I was a junior in High School and I was at a party at Nancy Blum's house I met this nice boy, Chuck (Randy) Dooly, he boarded and was schooled at Girard Collage a military school for boys without fathers. I was having the best time, suddenly, I had a little tickle in my head, I scratched, and there in my finger nail was a cootie. I was very upset; I called my Mother, told her of the bug. I stated I wanted Dad to come and get me NOW. Well that was something else again; he was out driving Miss Pearl on her Friday night runs. Dad arrived as soon as Mom was able to track him down. When I got home I was carrying on. *How did I get bugs*? Mother broke the news gently, one of the younger children caught then in school.   We all shared the same comb with one another. I brushed, combed, and got the nit comb. The next day I got the burn stuff and washed all the bedding in Lysol then I took the young ones and did the hair thing with them. "This was just an **infection**" mom said; I said, "it was an **infraction** to me." I thought I would never see Chuck again. I was lucky, he got our phone number from Nancy Blum, (we had phone service that month) thank the Lord, or the almighty dollar. He called, and we courted for a while, I met his Mom and Stepfather one Sunday, not sure what happened, maybe the mom did not like something about me, or maybe as Chuck explained to me in a letter, he did not want to get married, he had to go to college to become a Lawyer. **Married!** I thought to myself, I was just ending my junior year of school, I sent him a letter, asking where did he get such an idea? He said I was telling him how my friend **Joan O'Neil** was going to be married as soon as she graduated from High School, (and she did). I explained to him I was just telling him about her wedding, but we never went out again, I don't know if it was her wedding, the bugs, or his mom. I often wonder if he went on to law school and became a lawyer. I never read any stories in the paper of defenders or prosecutors by his name, but in October 2013, I saw a death notice in the Philadelphia Inquirer. The name was Charles (Chuck) R. D...... age 69. I said a prayer for my old friend Chuck; the death notice did not mention Esq. next to his name. I wonder what his occupation turned out to be?

My friend Jo's first hair cut

When my friend and I were sixteen, we saw a new hair style in a magazine. It was called *the bubble*. Jo had very long dark silky hair, almost to her shoulder blades or longer. She had purchased the hair style magazine, and she showed me **the bubble cut.** I liked it too, but your hair, had to be straight, for that style. Mine was already short and curly. Jo wanted her hair to look like the one in the book. Her mom wanted it the way it was. Well, by now, I tried biking, running, piano, singing, why not hair styling? I told her, I think I can do it for you. Mrs. S would never let her have a haircut, maybe just a trim to her bangs. Jo got the scissors and the comb. We headed for my back yard and did it. I cut and cut. I thought her hair was growing as I cut. It took forever. Halfway through, I knew we made a big mistake. At last I finished, it was short, up to her neck. I got the curlers out, wet the hair, sprayed, and set it. When it dried, I brushed it out and teased the hair doo. I had to admire my new-found profession. But when Jo got home her mom and dad were very upset to say the least. They sent her up to 5th and Olney to one of the better hair stylist, to trim it up and finish what I started. Now through the years the only hair I have continued to cut, were granddaughter's bangs (taped them down and followed the tape for a straight cut). I do, from time to time, trim my husband's hair around the ears, in between trips to the barber shop I also tackle my own hair, if I cannot fit in a hair dresser appointment in a busy week. *I never hung out my stylist shingle, or a barber pole.*

THE REFUNDABLE GLASS BOTTLES

I wonder how many of us think back, and recall the quart and smaller glass pop, or beer bottles that would reap you a nickel for the quart size ones and two cents for the small ones? I will never forget my refund experience. It was some time about the early fifties. We rarely ever had phone service to our Gladstone exchange, if my parents could not afford to pay the phone bill, Ma Bell (Bell Telephone) the name of the phone company, then Ma would shut your phone off. Ma never saw much of my Ma's money. One day Mom had to reach my grandmom Weldon. She had a Baldwin exchange. Mother said to me, *"Take this nickel bottle to Hoagie's candy store, and get the nickel, and call grand mom for me.* The old man at the candy store said, *I will give you candy for the bottle, NO!* I explained I had to call my grand mom. We had a long discussion, about me picking out five cents worth the candy. Honestly, I do believe the devil was tempting me. *"NO, I must call my grandmother",* I argued. He said, *"You may use my phone to call her, and then you pick out the candy.* I dialed BA-6-6566 by now you can see the phone numbers were 7 digits. Anyway, her phone rang busy, I tried two more times, then Mr. Hoagie said, *"you pick out the candy and go home"*. I grabbed the bottle and bolted out the door. I went up to the Drugstore on the corner of Palethorp St. and Wyoming Avenue, Mr. and Mrs. Novak ran the Pharmacy, and Soda Fountain. In her very Jewish accent she asked, *"Vat can I do for you"*? I told her I needed the nickel to make a call. *Here my dear*, she handed me the nickel, *"make your call"*, now she lived behind the store, and did not trust kids in the store alone. I tried calling at least three times, Busy again and again. By now I forgot the reason I was calling grand. *"Now listen honey you pick out a nice candy bar"* (they were only a nickel back then) same size as the one that cost 89 cents at CVS now days. I was so tired of the busy phone, and finely I gave into temptation. That Hershey bar was so good. When I got home Mom asked, *"what did grandmom say?"* *"Oh nothing, her phone kept ringing busy"*. *"Well give me the nickel I will try later"*. If you could have seen the blank look on my chocolate cover face, as I stood there in front of mom with her hand out. No money no candy left to soften her up and no call to my grandmother. Mom was very upset with me, *"now I will have to ask*

Jacamo to let me use his phone". He was the Italian man who lived adjacent to our left. He did not like us coming into his spotless house. He let mom make the call, I guess it turned out OK, never the less that was the sweetest Hershey I ever ate. I guess all was forgiven by mom, because the question to grandmom was, could Billy and I be allowed to stay the weekend at grandmom' s house. *"Yes"* and when Friday came, we were on the trolley for a weekend of fun. As you know today the pop bottles are plastic and end up in the trash or if lucky, the city and towns get the citizens to recycle, someone is making a buck, but it is not the consumer.

Happy Days, Holidays and Sad Days

We Pys had many of all the above, where do I begin? While I was still in the lower grades, up to the eighth grade, we were a family of ten, eight children, with dad and mom. My parent's best friends were Peg and George Berg. They had five children; I was a bit older then the Berg gang. The family lived on the 600 block of Cornwall Street over in the Tioga section of the city. With a total of thirteen children and four adults, and not a lot of cash flowing, the two families would gather at one or the other's home once or twice a month. Dad would play his banjo and George would pull out his Harmonica or Accordion. As they gather in one of the two kitchens, the music played, and they would sing old songs. "Peg of My Heart", She'll be Coming Around the Mountain", When Your Old Wedding Ring Was New, and, I'm Looking over a Four-Leaf Clover. There were many more I just cannot remember them all. Now when I hear some of the old songs, I am back in the kitchen with our family. Dad and George drank beer Mom had a high ball and Peg, red wine. Kids had Pop or juice. A big meal would be prepared while the children ran in one door and out the other; I would have a book to read, or some homework with me. After much beverages, and a delicious meal the adults would play a game of cards. Time to go home, was always a trudge. If it was summer, it would be, "just get in the car." Winter, it meant finding everyone's hats, coats etc. Now while piling into the car, there would be laughing, crying screaming, for what reason, I did not know, until we or they would get home. Inevitably and always, we or they would have one of the wrong or an extra kid at the finale destination. This would mean one of the men would have to drive the extra child back to their home. It was always a Sunday, so an overnight stay was out of the question. Of course, whoever the driver was, be it Dad or George, they would have to come in and have one for the road. Nowadays the police would have them pulled over for a sobriety test, not back then. None of the woman drove in the forties and early fifties. Even if they did, Peg and Mom would have been in the same boat. Oh, the last song of the day would always be, Happy Times Are Here Again. They could really belt out the tunes. I think I mention George was also in the Dick Crain String Band, but most important George was my Dad's Captain it the US Army, I know he looked after dad while over in Italy

Thanksgiving Day was the only Thursday in the year that an extra special dinner was prepared and served. At the Py house, preparations always started early Wednesday evening. Dad and Mom would cut the celery and onions and sauté them in butter or margin, mix them in the squared cubes of bread with seasoning to make the stuffing for the Turkey. I know that chef's say, *"never stuff the bird beforehand,"* everyone did. I still do. No one in our families has gotten salmonella. While the preparation was going on my parents always had their wine glasses filled. Next came the homemade pumpkin pies and one deep dish apple pie. The pumpkins always had a little wine in the mix, just to give them an extra flavor. Dad would make homemade whipped cream to top off the pies. We still use the same recipe now. Here is dad's gift to you for your holiday pies.

"1 **pt. of Heavy Whipping Cream, 4 tablespoons of 10 X Confection, or regular sugar, 1 tea spoon of Vanilla. Put all in a cold mixing bowl and beat on high until the cream forms peaks. Don't over mix or you will turn it to sweet butter. After it is stiffly whipped, keep it in the refrigerator until ready to spoon on the pies." The best .**

Usually Thanksgiving Day, was just for family. This one Thanksgiving Dad went out for a while, we had no idea where he was going, but he did say set an extra place at the table. My father had a heart of gold, mom too, they always gave half of anything they had to the poor. They did not know it, but we were poor. When Dad returned home, he had three young girls with him, under the age of twelve. They were the Davis sisters. He went to St. Joseph Girls Home at 29th and Allegheny Ave. (now Mercy

Technical High School) to pick up one girl; he promised the nun at the home he would take a child to our house for a Thanksgiving Dinner. All most all the girls were farmed out for them to have a family type dinner on this special day. When dad got to the home to pick up his ward for the day, Sister told him she had three children left that had nowhere to go, Dad explained to Sister he had eight children of his own and would take just one child. Sister mentioned all three were sisters. He would not separate the three girls on this special Thanksgiving Day. We had a baker's dozen that year. About ten years ago, I found out the girls were three of eleven children, five of the girls were in St. Joseph Girls home and the six boys were put in St. Joseph Boys Home. I never asked what happened to the father, but the mother could not take care of all the children. It just happened that their uncle was a friend of my second husband John C. Lynch. It is no coincident that I met their uncle so many   years   later.

The Pys were grateful to have, our parents, and proud of who we are. All this was given to us by God. Not every Turkey day was a normal holiday, the traditional day changed on a yearly basis. When our small Py family of five were still enjoying

Thanksgiving dinner at grandmom Weldon's, dad would do his traditional prepping the night before, so when he arrived at the 27th street home, he already started his wine tasting celebration at our house. Grandmom was a very straight-laced person. She had the Turkey in the pan waiting for dad to get the stuffing ready and put it in the bird. Suddenly dad had his hand, and arm up the turkey's cavity, holding it with his other hand, and out the front door he ran. Dad headed down 27th St. to Summerset St., around to Taney St. with Grand mom and Uncle John chasing after him. Mom and I tried to follow but we only made it to the end of 27th at Summerset St., when we saw dad heading back toward grand mom's house with the old Tom in tack. They both ended up back on the porch in the 2800 block of N.27th St. My father stated, "I just wanted to give the old bird one last fly by, before he went to the oven. Uncle John being a US Army veteran got a gobble out of the trip. O did I say gobble, I meant chuckle. Mom, grand and my aunts did not appreciate such caring on or flying around. Being a Py, one never knew how a Thanksgiving eve, or day would play out. One year, when the family was too large to continue to celebrate dinner at grandmoms, and our old shed had just been converted to a modern cooking kitchen, Oh, it was still the same size as the shed, a very small cooking area. Not having much room to maneuver in the new kitchen, and never, having a good pot holder let alone two, (always using a worn-out dish towel) trying to get the bird out of the oven, not to mention the wine glasses were never empty, my parents dropped the hot roasting pan with the turkey sliding on the not so perfectly clean floor. All the juices for the gravy were mopped up and put out in the trash. The turkey was wiped off, they said we would not be able to have the nice brown skin to eat; one of the best part of the bird was the roasted skin. Mom was not prepared for this mishap. Lucky, Mrs. Gerger lived in the rear of her store, and cooked at home that day. I always had to be the one to do the bidding for them, if they ran out or forgot something, and her store was closed. I reluctantly was sent to knock on her side door for whatever they needed. *"Happy Thanksgiving Mrs. Gerger"* I said, *"yes"*! *"What do they need now"*? She blurted out in broken English. *"Three cans of chicken or turkey gravy please"* I said. My parents were still running a tab at her store (*the book again*). Now how awful, Unity Frankford canned gravy for Thanksgiving dinner, Yuk, it was not good on a regular dinner day. Although, my 3rd son Stephen and his wife Peggy Ann use's Heinz jar gravy every Thanksgiving, I bring corn starch with me, so I can use the drippings for homemade gravy.

Now the best and the worst Turkey day came after I was married to John Hopkins and had our own home and family. I had stopped over 2nd Street on Wednesday the eve of Thanksgiving not to miss the traditional stuffing of the bird. Dad was due home with the jug of wine from the state store, and the *TURKEY*, remember he worked just across the street and around the corner. The PA State Store as they called it back then, (now Wine and Spirits) was on 4700 block of Rising Sun Ave. just two streets away from our family home. Dad had the use of Jack's car because he was also running errands for Pearl and Jack. We waited and waited, work left out a 5:00 PM every night, 5:45, 6:30, 7:45PM, time was ticking by. This was not the norm for a holiday eve. Food had to be prepared, pies to be baked, *and the PA State Store shut at 9:00 PM sharp*. What would mom do if he did not get home with the wine and the turkey? It was just about 8:45 when dad walked in the door. I could tell he had a few. Mom was furious. He had the jug of wine in a brown bag. *"Bill; where's the turkey*?*"* mom cried out, *"Oh*

Maim, (he called her that, he knew it would get her going); pour me a glass of wine.". "Come on Bill what did you do with the turkey?" "We have to prep the stuffing and pies etc.". "Maim, get me a glass of wine". Mom did as he asked, sat, and had some with him. She started getting anxious, she keep up the inquisition, so he got up, and started for the front door. The younger siblings were eager to help with the bird. My father, went to the rear of Jack Kenny's car opened the trunk, and up popped a **LIVE Turkey.** "O my God", my mom called aloud**. It was not God**; it looked like a bird to me. My father had the feather friend on a leash. Dad lifted it out of the vehicle and proceeded to parade the gobbler up and down 2nd Street. My younger sisters and brothers were jumping and laughing while chasing after dad and the fowl. Mom was frantic; she never killed an animal in her life and did not know the plucking process. What was she to do in this dilemma? *"Mom"*, I reminded her the brother's, Bill and Joe, now US Navy men were stationed at the Philadelphia Navy Yard while the ships were in for repairs. I said, *"Call the ship yard, and see if they can get a cook from the galley to help"*. "Oh" mom said, *"what a clever idea."* It worked, but not only Bill and Joe arrived, they brought half the US Navy

Fleet of men with them. After the defenders of our country finished off the only gallon of wine mom waited half the evening for, Bill took the bird to his basement till early AM then they put the Tom in the car and off to the chopping block, I have to say, Lyndon Baines Johnson did not give this bird a presidential reprieve. The turkey went down just after 4:00 AM November 27, 1964 and was back in our kitchen by 6:00 AM, ready to be stuffed and put in the oven on time. Mother had to bother Jacamo, the Italian next-door neighbor, who had a wine cellar; he made his own Italian wine. She asked for a jug of wine for our big day. Jacome came through **See the art on this story in back of the book.**

Everything went well, except my seven younger brothers and sisters would not have Tom for dinner, they ate HOT DOGS. They boycotted my parents for putting TOM the TURKEY down. We never found out where dad got the old bird. Did he go to a farm and fetch it, catch it, or I hate to think stole it, I guess I, and the rest of the clan will have to wait until we fly like a bird through the Pearly

Gates of Heaven, maybe dad will give us the answer to his turkey story? Billy and Marian know now! There were other Holiday stories Christmas ones are happy and sad. I am just getting started.

Christmas-Days.

I already gave you a tale of woe of one of my younger Christmas days. Now I can recall that our first Christmas on 2nd street was frugal. We were only in the home a month or so. I think my parents were literally getting their feet wet. Another new baby was on the way. Lots of bills had to be paid. Our Christmas tree was skimpy, as all Balsam trees are, (long, thin, and skimpy in the middle). They were the least expensive. Scotch Pines and Douglas Firs were perfect shape trees, Dad could not afford them, and neither could my first husband John and I, so for many years I had to be satisfied with a Balsam tree. In the beginning, I am not sure where dad acquired the tree from, but it never arrived at our house until very late Christmas Eve. This tradition went on for as long as Dad went by himself to fetch a tree. Maybe he acquired it after the tree merchants abandoned their post at the end of the night. This too, we will ask Dad when we see him again. He *is* noted for climbing fences. That is another tale to tell c.1959 yet to come. Santa did not bring me the walking doll that year. We did get underwear and socks. All our Christmas Dinners were a clone of the Thanksgiving Day dinners, except there were lots of candy canes all over the house, and on the tree. They were **FREE** at the War Memorial on the corner of Rising Sun and Wyoming Avenues, where Santa sat the Saturday before Christmas. He gave the mint canes out to all the kids, who waited in the long line to give Santa their wish list. Santa also handed out coloring books about himself and his reindeer. How proud Old St. Nick was of all his accomplishments. I still believed being told by mom, in 1949-50 or longer. Dad's grandfather the only **Pop** I knew, and **three** of his four daughters shared an inheritance of over $75,000.00. I never asked why my grandmother Meme was left out. Her pittance came much later, in fact not until after she passed away. Once more, as I mentioned before, *another person who did not have a will*. All ten of the Py kids (than adults) received her windfall through the blood line. It was a whopping $450.00 each, after our uncle, you know (SAM) got his demanding tax portion. Dad did not have a Will, and neither did Meme, so poor mom was left out without a reward. I tried offering mom my share, she would not take it. She said it was our inheritance. My $450.00 is still in the bank.

The reason I am explaining about the windfall inheritance that my Great grandpop Hoban and his gals received, is, that all four of them would send Mom a check at Christmas time. The purpose was to buy us children toys from St. Nick. Santa never brought many toys. I guess his bag would have been to heavy! It was always clothing, and food that was purchased, and a bill or two got paid down, they never got paid off, not till after dad died. I think my relatives felt guilty, since Mom was not welcome in the home on Napa Street. I never found out why. Eventually after great grandmom Maude (**nee Francis**) died. (I did not know about that either. Pop Hoban invited mom over to dinner. It was nice to be with both my parents at Sunday dinner. I never liked going without mom. I always asked why Mom did not come? But no one ever sad a word. I was never told much of anything. Mom would never hurt anyone. Someone must have had a bug in her bonnet, over something simple. (I do know, Maud wore her hair in a knot at the back of her head, always covered with a hair net. Maybe the old woman had a never-ending head ache? Something else I found out a few years ago, from my Aunt Catherine (Murphy) Curran Pop Hoban's fourth daughter, besides his four daughters, Pop adopted a son. I'm not sure if the boy had the Hoban name. I don't even know his first name. *Funny how they all kept secrets.* Dad grew up in Pop's house, he must have known his own uncle. My Father had brittle bones. If dad sneezed to hard, he would fracture a rib. He was always falling and breaking some part of his body. The year c 1954 they decided to hang new wall paper just before Christmas, Uncle John, and dad got as far as the hallway going up the stairs. Dad slipped, fell down the steps and broke his ribs. He was out of work over the holidays and another lean Christmas. In 1960, just past Thanksgiving we were getting ready, to spruce up the house for the holidays. On December 8th, Dad, Mom, Billy, and I had a project to paint, and stucco the living room, dining room and ceilings. I was working full time for an Insurance Agency. Dad was due home with the two gallons of paint @ $8.00 a piece, so we could get started, as to finish the job before Christmas. Now I will remind you it was a Friday. Dad did not do well on Fridays. My two younger sisters Pat and Marie had gone to a Girl Scout meeting. The rest of us were waiting- waiting and waiting for dad to come in the door. My sisters arrived home from Scouts about 9:15 PM. They reached our house before Dad. We had a Friday night tradition; all the younger children could stay up late since there was no school the next day. Mom always provided a treat for us on payday. The treats were ready; my sisters came in the door and went right to their bedroom. I said, *'Mom what's with the girls?"* No one knew. It was getting very late, and a light snow had begun to fall about an hour and a half before the girls arrived home. Mom and I figured dad was lost on one of his Friday night fiascoes. Suddenly, a knock on the door, two strangers were standing on our front porch. They inquired in broken English, as to our last name," *PY"* we said. We were informed, that a tall red headed man was lying in the snow-covered street around on Mentor. Dad told the Good Samaritans he was Bill Py and his address. He had not made it as far as Jack and Pearl's home. Dad fell short by about 150 feet, and flat on his back. He said, "he slipped in the snow"?? Need I say more? Yes, because, dad encountered the two Good Girl Scouts, just outside our house at 9:15 PM, he told them "If you two mentioned seeing me to mom, they would be in trouble." Well, we were all in the soup now. Mom had to get Bob Warman a neighbor to help get him home and into the house, dad could not stand on his legs, and claimed to be in a lot of pain. He was rushed to Germantown Hospital Accident Ward. It was determined he had one broken leg and fractured ankle on the opposite foot. Dad spent that Christmas in the hospital, and had lost his cash in a card game, so the money for the paint went up in smoke, and yes, I paid for the paint, with money that was my final layaway payment on a new dress. I was invited by a wonderful guy, to go on a special date with him to General Electric's employees Christmas party, on the following Friday night, I lived on a rigid budget and that money, for the paint was from the last pay I would receive, before the night of my date. (A note of charity), my bosses noticed a change in my mood at work, this would not do, since I was the smiling voice on their phone at Wildemore Ins. Agency, so; when I was asked, *"why the gloom"* I explained my dilemma, Mr. Jake Wildemore Sr. gave me the $16.00 cash to get the dress from layaway and put a smile back into their business. Yes, we did get the house ready for our very humble Christmas, and I had a grand time on my first and only date with Tom Hellfinger on Dec. 15th.

It was the first and only date, of many first and only ones. I wonder why? Christmas morning was here, after we went to Mass and had a holiday breakfast; Mom called Yellow Cab Co. and all eleven of us pilled in the cab. The driver kept asking how many more had to get in his cab? (This would not happen if we called an UBER today). We went to see Dad at the Hospital, just one problem, no visiting children under twelve were allowed in his hospital room. The younger kids and I went around to the side window to peer in at Dad. Thank the Lord he was on the first floor. I can just imagine me hoisting one at a time up to a higher window, what one won't do for parental love. There are more broken bones stories, but this is all for the Christmas ones.

Backtrack, I can tell you about something around the 4th of July 1959. I returned from a two-week trip to Colorado Springs with the Girl Scouts, I got back to Philadelphia 30th Street Train Station on the following Saturday, Dad was to pick me up in Jack's car. I looked for him, but I saw our neighbor Bob Warman, (he seemed to always be picking up a Py) *"Hi PY"* he said to me, come on I will take you home. There was no conversation on the thirty-minute ride home. All kinds of thoughts wandered in my brain. We arrived at my front door; Bob took my things into our home. There was my dad in a hospital bed in our dining room. The truth of the matter was, on or about the 4th of July, Local 19 ran a picnic, my brothers won a ball, while they were playing with it, the ball went over a high chain link fence topped with bobbed wire. Dad having fun, and a few beers climbed the fence retrieved the ball, climbed back over, but did not clear the hedge at the bottom of the fence. He fell and broke both legs. Dad was back in the hospital bed in the dining room, this time in a full body cast for almost a year. Instead of Bill he should have been named *Bones, broken to be exact.*

My life in Cardinal Dougherty High School

September 1956 this brand new and, largest Catholic High School on the East Coast opened its doors for the first time. (Unfortunately, this magnificent school is now closed after only 54 years). Over 1,600 freshmen, and 1,000 sophomores from the appointed feeder schools entered this brand-new institute of Catholic education.

The school was divided into a girl's side and the boy's side, and NEVER were we to meet, except for afternoon (mixers-dances) or evening dances. The immense cafeteria had a wall between the two sides of the building. The school was co-educational, but in its incubation period girls and boys were not joined in the classrooms. CD was run as if it were two separate schools, except for Mass which was held in the vast auditorium. Co-educational classes did not begin until the year c.1983. My two youngest sons, Stephen and Michael were one of the first in our family to be in a co-ed classroom. When I attended CD while during lunch periods, in the early days if one of the doors between the two sides opened, and the boys would whistle and make (Woo) sounds at the girls, or vice versa it would be mass punishment for all involved. Other than the strict rules we had to follow, It was the finest school and I had the time of my life for the four years I attended CD.

On the opening day, all girls went to the girl's gym and the boys were sent to theirs. Roll call started, and each person was assigned to a home room.

This new experience had my complete attention; I did not want to miss anything. Names of girls were called over the sound system, and I heard the name Nancy Mottson, and I jutted down her home room number, could this be one of my old friends from Swampoodle? The nun in charge continued to recite names and rooms, once again I recognized another name, and further done the alphabet Kathleen Tyrell. I was beside myself, here I am in yet another new school, years later and now I am reconnected with some of my young childhood friends. Our school still needed some finishing touches, so in the beginning we had half days. As the first day ended, and we were dismissed, I took off to locate the girls that just might be my old friends. Yes, as I found each one, they were the girls that lived on 28th street near Clearfield. We were reunited in high school and stayed in contact during the next four years. I was elated. This new experience was going down in my book. (*The one I had no idea I would write at the time),* it was just an expression.

During our first year at CD we only had six subjects and no lunch or study period. While the school needed the additional work, so all the offices would be equipped adequately, we were dismissed by 12:30 PM each day for almost the entire year. I tried out for the CD Drill Team, what a farce that was. I did not have that so called *drily smile*, let alone, I was not a thin girl and would never been able to lift my legs as high as the girls on the drill team could. With that defeat, I decided to fall back on my second-grade singing skills and tried out for the Glee Club. What a synch. I made it. No! I was never a soprano or even second soprano; I landed in the alto section. My voice is the one God gave me, and it was and is what it is, deep and chirpy. People always ask me, "Are you from, New York, or Boston or some other state in the North"? *"NO"* I would say, *"Just Philadelphia,"* we seem to have a language (twang) of our own.

My scholastic marks remained just passing in my freshman year. I still do not know how I passed Algebra or Latin, but no summer school for me. Thank heavens, because I had to keep that job at the 5 & 10 store to defray my carfare, and book bill at CD. Back in the olden days (by the way if you are twenty-one or younger now, *this is your olden days*), just remember that years from now. Anyone my age or younger knows there was no such thing as tuition in the Catholic School system. The parishes flourished with large families and church going people. Today is quite a different story. No Cardinal Dougherty High School. The last graduation class was 2010; by the way my grandson Kevin Patrick Hopkins was in the class of 2009. Parish schools and churches in and around the city of Philadelphia are closing all the time. No one knows until it is too late to help support a doomed school or church. Besides, the fact is Catholics are jumping ship, either not going to church or joining other churches, not staying with the *Rock that God gave to St. Peter, "Upon this Rock I will build My Church"*

Well I made it to sophomore year, and sang my way through, I even went to the Sophomore Hop, grandmom Weldon made me a beautiful moss green tea length dress, and I took Bob Blair, a boy I met at a LaSalle High School Dance, they opened their dances to the girls from other Catholic schools since LaSalle was an all boy's school, and they needed girls to attend. (Now days things are changing, and not for the good). Bob was also a sharp dresser, and he thought he was the coolest guy around. I don't know what he saw in me, but he was around during that entire year. Oh, get this, I had to be home by 10:30 PM. Everyone else were going out for a snack after the dance, but not the PY girl, so home I was at 10:30 on the dot. I was obedient to the end. Junior year, still with the glee club, and my marks were better than ever, it was the St. Joseph nuns, not saying the other order of nuns were not good. I was just used to St. Joseph nuns as a little girl, you know the one in the long black gown with the big whit bib, and I still wasn't sure if any of them had ears or hair? But those eyes in back of their heads, got you all the time.

Mother was pregnant in 1958-59 due to have our tenth slice of the PIE, I being so young and naïve was a little mortified or maybe more. None of my friend's moms were always having baby's year after year, just my mom. The baby was due in late March; this would be Regina (Jennie), and so was my Junior Prom coming up in April, Mother told me early on, we do not have the money for you to be able to attend the prom. My book bill of $20.00 was not yet paid and the end of the school year was approaching. I resigned myself I would not be able to attend this event.   March 30, 1959 mother entered Nazareth Hospital to have this baby girl. In those days expectant mothers would go to the hospital when the child was on the way and they stayed for a full week to recoup. While Mom was still in the hospital, Jo's cousin Billy S…who also was a junior at CD needed a date for the prom. He was one of two children, his brother Bob, & himself. I had already dated his older brother Bob, who by the way went on to be a doctor. Back to the prom, what luck, I could attend the prom, and I did not need any money, before I accepted his invite I had to use the next-door neighbors phone to call mom in the hospital and ask permission. *"NO, you may not go to this prom"*, was mom's answer. Did I dare ask why, yes, I did? *You will need a dress, shoes and God knows what else,* (I was thinking **and maybe a bra that fit me, that I could call my own**. With mothers last word. I hung up the phone and started out of Jacamo's dining room. Just than his phone rang, I stopped; hopping it was mother changing her mind. Not mom, but my Aunt Dot, (they all had the neighbors phone number in case of an emergency). Mr. Morrittizo called me back and handed me the receiver. Aunt Dot was asking about her sister (mom) and the new baby girl. I know my voice was low and sad. Aunt Dot, my big best friend and mentor wanted to know what was wrong. I poured out my heart to her. *"No problem, I will call your mom and tell her, I will take care of all your needs"*, I asked shyly, **"and can I get a brassiere too"? She laughed, she apparently did not know, I had been wearing second hand bras of mom's, (Like in a song about "Second hand Rose") Mom received the news over the phone and called to tell me I could accept the invitation to the junior prom. All this being settled, and my relief** overflowing, when I went to school the next day, the home room nun talked about what type lady like dresses, and the shoes the girls should ware to the dance. *"Remember now"* she stated, *"no Patent Leather shoes, they reflect up."* All the girls laugh. At that time no one knew there would be a Broadway Show in NY City about the Patent Leather Shoes. It was, and still is a musical comedy on how the nuns took on all those quirks. *"Miss Py, I know you will not be attending this event, because you have not paid your book bill yet."* I never talked back to anyone, but she had just embarrassed me in front of the whole home room class. I gently rose from my desk, stood next to it, or I should say leaned on it, because for the first time I would speak back to a woman in a holy habit. *"Yes Sister"* I stated, *"as a matter of fact, I will be attending my junior prom"*. "Oh" she went on *"how do you plan to make that happen, when you still owe the studies office the unpaid $20.00 book bill"*, and then she waived a black book at me. OH! that darn BOOK again, will I ever forget it, will it ever go away? *"Well Sister, I was invited by a junior from the boy's side and he is paying for the prom tickets, and all that goes with the event"*. She just stared at me; I waited and held on to the desk, I thought I was doomed. *"Be seated"*, *"you tell your parents they owe this money, do you hear me"*. **"YES SISTER"** I sort of sang back to her that famous chant we would answer all the nuns with. To me, it seems no one cared that my mom was in the hospital and had just given birth to her tenth child. We did not know if we would have electricity, at times. But the nun wanted that $20.00. Aunt Dot took care of all I needed, I looked and felt wonderful. I went to the prom with Bill S my friend Jo's cousin, a post prom gathering at Drew Green's house, and home by 1:00 AM. What a wonderful memory, everyone should attend all their school dances. I never had another date with Bill. If I am correct, I don't think he ever married. He took care of his parents. Since I can't get Jo, my friend to respond to any of my correspondence, I could be mistaken about Bill. Prior to our junior school year ending CD held many mixers (dances) in the girl's gym. Not the boy's gym, because it was a solid wood floor for the basketball team. On one of our last Friday evening dances that year 1959, Jo, and I, as usual were hugging the wall, when the master of ceremony announced a lady's choice, it was a slow dance. We had our eyes on two guys all night; they were not dancing with any one special, so we decided to ask them to dance.

She took the tall one (Andrew Farley) I asked the other boy, who by the way had a very nice, but BROWN suit on. As I tapped him on the shoulder immediately he introduced himself to me. *"Hello, I am John C. Lynch from Presentation BVM parish in Cheltenham"*. Boy was that a mouthful. With that, I repeated, to him; *"I am Elaine B. Py, from Incarnation of Our Lord Parish in the Olney section of Philadelphia"*. He then said, *"Oh! an Inky girl"*. I wondered what was wrong with that? As I answered *"Yes"*. Maybe I should have waited this one out, I thought to myself. When the waltz was completed it was about 9:00 PM, all four of us stood around and chatted for a while, John keep his eye on the clock. I asked *why are you so involved with what time it is? The dance is not over until 10:00 PM.* He stated, *"any student that came to the dance had to stay until 9:30PM"*, he was gone by than; he had to catch a bus or something. Well here I was shot down, before I got a running chance. On Monday, while in home room, a girl Carol R said, *"I saw you dancing with John C. Lynch Friday night"*. *"Yah"* I said in a very low voice. Carol told me he had a steady PUBLIC girlfriend. That was that, (senior year will come later).

The next time I saw John C. Lynch was at our

Cardinal Dougherty ten-year reunion in1970, I was the President of the Alumni Association for CD, myself and a committee of men and women put together this reunion. I, being the President, had to give out some prizes, one of which was a bottle of red wine, it was to be presented to the first student from our class of 1960 that had married and was first to have a baby. It was John C. Lynch, the boy, now the man in still a **brown suit**; he and his wife had a little girl Lorrie, I did get to know and love her later in my life .(Lorrie died 3/28/16). John had joined the Marine Corps in September 1960 he had been a Marine for four years. After completion of his enlistment, he became a Municipal Police Officer for Cheltenham Township Police Department. John completed twenty-nine years with them; and his wife Janet E. (Ade) Lynch was able, through an associate, to secure an application for John to be a Federal Police Officer. He was accepted by the Government because of his police background and tenure as a municipal police officer. In 1995 John started his second career with the United States Treasury as a police officer working for the United States Mint. He quotes "*I was watching all your money.*", . He stayed in that position for 12 years. He retired at age 65 on

September 30, 2007. (John C. Lynch Day in Cheltenham, PA.) I know he is enjoying this well-deserved retirement, **why do I know all this**? first because my deceased husband John T. Hopkins liked John C. Lynch and followed JC's career along with his K-9 dogs from 1983 up until John T. died on November 30, 1999 .J C was at the US Mint by then .And most of all because with the love of my God, and faithfulness to our Cardinal Dougherty Alumni Association, after the death of both our loving spouses, John C. Lynch and I, Elaine B. (PY) Hopkins, the girl from Inky, (not too shabby now)? is Mrs. John C. Lynch, married to **the boy in the brown suit**. I will tell you a truth, of what I thought was love, and then of my first true love, John T. Hopkins, I will let you know how I became one of "The Lovely Lynch's "as J. C. often refers to when speaking of his family.

thinks

Lynch,
brown

family.
Sometimes he he is so cool??

.

J   C
the boy in the suite. CDHS

Climbing the steps of infatuations and, love-to-Heartache

Late winter of 1958, I met the nicest looking fellow, tall, blondish hair and really a stylish dresser. Now I thought I knew what love was. His name was Tom Mc D...... I say **was** because it changed, (The truth to be told later) he is still alive, and I think still a good looking older gent 76 to be exact. He recently, October 2013, asked if he was going to be in this story. I said *yes, but Tom you may not like what you read. He said to me, "It is what it was, so it's OK to print what happened."* The way we met back then is not the way girls should meet boys today. I was working in S.S. Kresge 5&10 at Germantown and Lehigh; I started there when I was 15. Jo and I needed jobs, and our neighborhood 5&10 in Olney had no openings, so they sent us to one of their other stores in North Phila. We took public transportation PTC to and from the job. To get home, we would take the # 23 trolley car, a very long ride up to Windrum Ave. and the 75 trackless over east Wyoming Ave. to our respective streets. One night while waiting for the trolley, a big sedan pulled up to the curb and the boy sitting in the passenger invited us in, the two fellows wanted to give us a lift home. We both said no thanks and continued to wait for our transportation home. We boarded the #23 PTC, (now SEPTA) trolley car but, noticed the big sedan was right alongside it. Back than the windows of the transit vehicle could be raised and lowered. The guys kept calling out to us. We avoided them and moved to the opposite side of the trolley. We arrived at the stop where we had to exit, and board a trackless #75 car going E. to Wyoming Ave., there they were waiting at the corner at Wyndrom and Germantown Ave. "Come on, let us take you home"? We tried to evade them and got on the trackless toward home. Their vehicle stayed right with us. "Oh my", "what are we going to do" we asked each other? We cannot let them follow us to our homes. Jo would get off at 3rd and my stop was at 2nd street. We both decided to get off at 5th street so they would not know where we lived. "Aw come on; let us get you two a soda pop? When Jo saw the driver of the car, she liked what she saw, a very good looking Italian fellow (she is half Italian) and I thought (Tom) was cute, so we made a deal, we told them where the soda shop was, and if by the time we would walk there, if they were there, we would go in and have a soda with them. It was a good two blocks to 3rd and the Roosevelt Blvd. We bet each other they would not be at the Pizza shop, and we could just head home. We arrived at Luciano's Pizza in five minutes, and the car was parked right outside the store. Jo and I went in and met Vince, he was the driver and Tom a mutt, part Irish and Lithuanian. They told us they lived in the Nicetown area near Germantown Ave. They usually hung out at Whiteys Diner but decided to cruise down the avenue this night. I must say surprisingly to Jo and me, both were perfect gentlemen. (Today if a girl took a hop, in a stranger's car it just may be trouble with a capital T) That was the first of many times we were in their company. Jo and I continued to see them but did not know what to tell our parents as to how, and where we met.? Somehow, we got past the how's. Vince stopped coming around, Jo never got a reasonable answer. Tom would visit me at least two or three times a week whenever possible. I think he told me he worked at the Inquirer building on N. Broad Street at nights, getting the morning papers bundled for morning delivery. My parent's phone was shut off again, so there was no way for he and I to communicate with each other, unless he would call me over at Jo's house at a certain time on a specific day or night. It was now June and school was out, Tom would come strutting down 2nd street from getting off the R bus on a balmy summer night, I was in my glory. We really liked each other. I believe at the time, he was my first Love. I mentioned before about the trip to Colorado with the girl scouts, well while I was on the train the first evening, of a three-day trip out, I met many girls from different areas of Philadelphia. We had a hilarious incident happen, when the PA train stopped in Pittsburgh, PA to connect two coaches of a train that came from NY transporting other girl scouts to join the Reading Train. While in the train yard waiting for the connecting cars to be coupled on, there was a train on the track directly across from our coach, it had a Pullman compartment in the middle of the passenger train. The shades to the sleeper were **up** and what we saw from our windows was a man in the upper birth lying there in his **Birthday Suit,** if you know what I mean. He was reading a book. We all started telling others (it was like whisper down the lane) and everyone from other compartments were streaming into our area; it's a wonder our compartment did not topple over, everyone started giggling, then laughing aloud etc. The man must have senced eyes on him, abruptly he pulled the shade. It must have been the first time most of us ever saw a naked man. As the chaperons tried to resume order and get the girls into their proper area, I met Susan, a gal from the Germantown, Nicetown section of Philadelphia. We started chatting, and I told her about my boyfriend Tom McD, who hailed from her neighborhood. Susann stated she knew almost all the boys from Whitey's Diner, and there was no one with that name. **She must be wrong**, I thought. I persisted with her, and finely showed her his photo. My first disappointment, his name was Tom, but not Mc Donald as she proceeded in telling me, his real last name Sav… or something like that. This trip, I was looking forward to for so long, had now turned into a nightmare on a train to hell the first night out. What was I to do? My so-called boyfriend had lied to me, and I could not reach him for an explanation. (Did I want to? Yes) I was so hurt and embarrassed. I had to put my dilemma on the back burner until the second week in July when I would return home; (HOME was to be a happy place to come to, safe from harm) I was not looking forward to my arrival) Tom had given me his so-called address, and he had my section and address in Colorado. That night on the train I could not sleep, so I wrote a letter to him. **This was the first of many letters during our** *relationship.* I did not mention my encounter with Susan and I addressed the letter to Tom McDonald. (By the way much later after fifteen-years of marriage to John T. Hopkins, I met Jimmy McDonald, Tom's best friend'. Jim married the girl who lived next door to our home on Tampa St. Jim was a good ten years older than Jessica, but love forms for all ages. Jimmy was putting aluminum siding on our property. As I sat in the front of the house, I talked while he worked. A conversation of Whitey's Diner came up, and I told Jim a story about Tom. To my astonishment, and Jim's, it was the same Tom. Jim made one statement, I never forgot, *"So you are the girl Tom went out of the neighborhood for."* Then he said, (*"I may have done the same back than if I knew you."*) (Jim is now deceased, and Jessica left a widow.)

Our train arrived in Chicago for a day stop, I mailed my letter. Three days later, upon arrival in Pikes Peak, Co., after setting up, we had mail call, I could not believe it, I was the first one to receive mail. There was a letter from home, and one from Tom. There had to be a mistake about his name. I will settle it when I returned to PA. A wonderful experience had come to an end and we were on our way home. Upon arriving at the 30th station, and being picked up by Bob Warman, then home to find Dad in that hospital bed again, the Tom thing was now secondary in my world. Two days passed, and I settled back to my regular routine. Giving Mom more support and going back to my part time job, I did not think of 'Tom. Tuesday night, while sitting on my front stoop, I look up toward Roosevelt Boulevard, there he was strutting down Second Street. My heart jumped and sunk at the same time, glad to see him, but how do I approach him with a lie between us? A little kiss in public was appropriate. Then I sat him on the corner store stoop, I did not want Mom to know all this mess. I came right out looked him in his eyes with tears in mine and told him what I found out while on the train. YES, he knew Susan, and NO his name was not Mc Donald. He was using his best friend Jim's last name and address. If my memory is correct? he claimed to be ashamed to tell me his last name Z…., and that he lived in a big rented Brown Stone apartment in the Spring Garden section of the city with his, I think he said, step mom and dad. Why fib to a Py girl? I lived in a small row home in Olney or Feltonville and we had out grown our home four or five years ago. I was not ashamed of my family, home, or heritage. I believed his tale about his name, and family. We continued seeing each other and would walk to a nearby park, on nights when he was broke, (no cash) for a movie, or bowling. We had a certain tree we would sit under and talk about a lot of things, mostly the future, my upcoming senior year in high school, and my prom. Then we would make out. It was always Tom that did not want to stop, so we would end up quarreling and walked back to my home. When this happened, I would think, **well I will never see him again**. Weeks would come and go, and we would repeat the same walk and fight all over again. How far was too far? Now it was a threat, but I did not want to lose him, our last trip to the park, I decided this was it. I would not stop him. We began to kiss etc. when it came time, I did not say NO, he proceeded to unbuckle his belt, I had tears in my eyes, I prayed to God, *"please Lord, help me, I do not want to do this, but I don't want to lose him."* At that exact moment, he got up started to buckle up, and kissed my cheek, and told me he could not hurt me, and how much he respected my virginity and faith in God. We walked home not speaking to each other. He left and said see you in a bit? I always worked at the 5&10 on Monday, Wednesday, Friday nights and all-day Saturday. I never missed work and Tom never asked me on a date on those nights. This one Saturday late summer I had a toothache, I called out of work, Jo was not scheduled to work that day. Once I saw the dentist, I was feeling better, so she and I decided to go to the Logan Theater on Broad Street, just past Wyoming Ave. It has long since been torn down. One of the newest movies was showing. *"A SUMMER PLACE"* staring Sandra Dee and Troy Donahue. We were looking forward to a nice night out just two friends. This movie theater had a balcony, mostly used for lovers. Jo and I sat in seats floor level with the screen, we were involved watching the love seen. The actors were matched well together. I, for whatever reason, turned and looked up in the balcony, this one couple were really going at it. Their love seen was better than the one in the motion picture. As I continued to watch them, suddenly, I thought I recognized the male to be no other than my Tom. This couldn't be him, **or** could it be? The theater always had a short intermission back then; people would use the rest rooms or get popcorn during the pause. At the intermission the male got up and left the balcony. I got up, told Jo I would be back with a treat, she did not follow me. I reached the lobby, there he was, my boyfriend, **the one I would have done anything for?** Now it certainly looked to me he had another girl, *maybe one that put out for him*? I was so upset, I backed up, pulled myself together, best I could, and returned to my seat with the popcorn. I never told Jo this part of that evening. I just continued to watch the rest of the show. I fooled around after the movie, so we would not be leaving, and running into the loving couple. Now here I was again for a second time, faced with what looked to me as outright deceit. The following Tuesday, as I sat outside my home pondering what a fool I have been. Who showed up on the corner of my street but Tom? He walked up to me like he owned the **WORLD** and **ME**. "Hi sweetie" he said, *"how was work this past weekend"*. I again, came out with the truth, as I know what I saw at the theater. He was stunned not to mention, he could not think fast enough to tell an outright lie, so I thought! He was caught. He told me her name was *Barbara* R...... an old friend from his real neighborhood Spring Garden, (now called Fairmount) not the Hunting Park area where he hung his hat... He said, "**She** invited him to the movie, and since I was working, he decided to go out with her, after all we weren't engaged". When I questioned him about the bat session I saw in the balcony, he told me it was all her, and since she paid to get in, he felt obligated to give into her wishes. With doubt, I bought his story, hook, line, and sinker. I did not want to believe the *truth*, as to what I saw. I cared for him too much to lose him. We took our usual walk, talked, kissed good night and he said I will see you soon. ***BOY IS LOVE BLIND***? Remember, our phone was always shut off for lack of payment, so I would have to *wait* until Tom would show up. He at this time did not work at the Inquirer anymore, so I could not call him in the evening like I use to, from Jo's phone or a pay phone, (try to find a pay phone now days).

Two weeks passed, Tom arrived in a car, this one Sunday afternoon, he was again the passenger in his friend Jimmy Walsh's dad's car. This was out of the norm. He never came on a Sunday. We, Jo and I, Tom and Jimmy took a ride to Greenwood Dairy in Langhorne, PA, for ice cream, we shared The PIG'S Dinner, you older people know what that was, (Ice cream served on a large board there would be all flavors of ice cream, and all the fruit and nuts, smeared with chocolate syrup, and covered with whipped cream). We finished the ice cream and started down Roosevelt Boulevard toward home.

On the way home I was so happy, the car radio played "Put you head on my shoulder" and I did, it was than he told me he joined the Army. He would leave before my 17th birthday September 15th. It was join or be drafted. He did not have a job so there was no other option. Once again, I was disappointed. My last year of High School, Senior Prom and my guy would be somewhere far away. We got home at dinner time and I had to leave him, **he promised to write me, and I promised to wait for him until he got discharged from the service, and that I would write every night.** I kept my promises, wrote to him almost every day, he sent a few letters when he could. Basic training left no time for a soldier to write much, *so I thought*. I had a friend Jackie K…. that fixed me up with a date for the senior prom. No one should ever miss **the last dance**. I had a wonderful evening with Danny Morrison. He lived right up the street at 2nd and the Boulevard, he was Jackie's neighbor. My prom was my first and last date with Danny; he was just a date   for   prom   night.

Tom was stationed at Fort Dix, NJ Army Station, (Now Joint Fort Dix-Maguire Air Base) and he asked if I would try to come over to see him before he would leave for Germany, it was late June of 1960. I had graduated High School and working full time for Wildmere Insurance Agency, in Olney on N. 5th Street. Even though I was earning money, and most of it I handed over to Mom to help support our family. I was still 17 and obedient to my parents. How would I pull this off, Fort Dix was far, and I would have to go to center city and then a NJ Transit bus over to the base? If I asked mom or dad, the answer would be NO. So, I made up a story, *a lie*, I never lied to mom and dad; this was the only way I could see him before he shipped out. I told them I was going to Harrisburg on a bus trip with Pat C…... the girl I worked with. They believed my story, so off I went. It was a long trip back then. The bus drove very slowly, and I was afraid. Finally, I arrived, Tom met me, and we had lunch, we walked and talked, and he gave me an Army ring. I was his girl. When I boarded the bus for Philadelphia, I was full of joy, and guilt, because I deceived my parents. Mom asked, "Did you have a wonderful day"? I did, so that was no lie. Time passed, and I got over my guilt. I was still working part time at the five and ten on Germantown Ave. We need the money. I would get mail from Tom, maybe one or two in a three-week's time, he was still at Fort Dix... I lived for the mail man to deliver a letter from him. Mom told me, to go out with other guys while he was away. *"No! I have a ring from him, and I am waiting for him that is that" I stated.* I am recalling this one Wednesday night; the memory will stick with me forever. I was at work at the 5 & 10 store, a girl came up to my counter. She had a box of white hankies, a pen and pencil set, and a box of writing paper to pay for. As usual, the chatty person I am, I asked, *"Do you write a lot of letters"*? She stated, *"No"*, it was for her boyfriend, he was in the Army, I told her so was mine. She continued talking while I wrapped her purchase. She told me he was on hold at Fort Dix, I laughed and said, *"so is my boyfriend at Fort Dix, and he is waiting to go to Germany"*, I said "maybe they know each other", although how likely could that be at such a large Army Base? *"What is you beau's name"*? *"Tom"* she said, I choked out a laugh, and told her *"so is mine (Tom)"* *"what's his last name"*? Z…. she stated proudly. Immediately my laugh turned to tears, as I informed her, *"So is my boyfriend's last name Z….* I handed her the package, I was shaking, and trying to stay in control, after all I was at work. She just stood there in shock for the longest time. She managed to tell me her name, **Barbara R…**; she was just as stunned as I was. Then I remembered, (*the girl in the balcony of the movie theater was also named Barbara R, she was one in the same*). I introduced myself and we agreed to meet on Friday night at her home after I finished work. She lived at 10th and Brown St. in the Spring Garden part of town. I had to again lie to my parents, as to why I was going to be late getting home from work that night. We met and went to her bed room to talk, out of reach of her father's ear. When I saw her stack of letters and the Fort Dix Pillow, photos, and the same Army ring on her dresser, I knew it was over for Tom and I. Barbara and I parted on friendly terms, I wished her luck. I think she was going to need it. When I arrived home, mom told me I received a letter from Tom. I took it to my room, wrote on it **RETURN TO SENDER** and posted it back to him on Saturday. I kept receiving mail from him for the next three years. I continued to send his unopened letters back. Mom was **right about me seeing other fellows. Mom was always right**. I started going out, and met, and dating other guys, three to be exact. What I thought was **love**, was just puppy love; a summer romance for a couple of teenagers. Note: Tom, signed my CDHS year book, "*Good Luck. Hope We Have a Nice Summer, LOVE TOM Z*

"SMACK whatever smack means, I forgot to   ask. Some words used in a popular song and Broadway show "The Sound of Music, now come to my mind, "You are sixteen, I am seventeen" *that is all we were.*

My True Loves (Were always in front of me, and   I   did   not   know   them.
Jo and I walked to 5th & Olney Ave. a lot in our youthful days. Not much else to do, when there was not money to spend. There this one fellow who always seemed to be around. We first saw him as an usher in St. Helena Church, at the viewing of Cardinal Dougherty's principal Fr. Concannon. This older than I person was always dressed in a suit, tie, and a tan trench coat. He seemed to be someone of *importance.* I did not know how important he would be in my life, back while I was still a high school girl? When JFK was running for president of the United States of America, everyone wanted a glimpse of the young handsome Democratic candidate. Jo, and I waited at 5th and the Boulevard as Kennedy's motorcade was due to pass on route to center city. While standing out on the Boulevard for over an hour, a group of young adults came to the intersection, and we noticed this fellow from St.

Helena's church, still wearing his trench coat, and always a white shirt and tie, this time he was wearing a straw hat, the hatband was printed John F. Kennedy for President. We found out this fellow was the president of the Young American Democrats for JFK.

John T. Hopkins was also on the lips of a lot of the girls from St. Helena's parish, who I associated with at CD. I would hear them say, "Oh did you see Hoppy last night? Or, "we had a pop with Hoppy at the corner soda fountain last night"; (it was located on 4th St. near Spencer). I often wondered, who was this Hoppy guy that all the girls talked about. After I graduated High School, the only dances we could go to until you reached drinking age, were held at a place on Roosevelt Blvd. called **Brookline Country Club.** Believe me when I say it was not a Country Club, it was the building adjacent to the old Boulevard Pools. If they felt good calling it a country club, so be it. The place worked for us under age nondrinkers. It was December 1961, and this person I saw all over Olney, while I was in high school, and during the campaign for John F. Kennedy for President, asked me to dance. I was flabbergasted to say the least. It was then I met John T. Hopkins, (Hoppy) He introduced himself as John T. Hopkins of St. Helena's parish in Olney. (**NOTE**) **how everyone associated themselves with their parish school and neighborhood.** The first dance never ended, we danced all night. The band leader directed the last waltz of the evening, it was "**Moonlight Serenade**, a Glenn Miller piece arranged by Jerome Thomas" **I'll never forget that night, it was magical for me.** Later that week, in work, as I mentioned dancing with him to Pat Casell, my co-worker, I found out he was notorious for dating a girl only twice, and then he would find a new girl to keep him company. It was mid-January 1962 when John T. Hopkins asked me to attend his church's **St. Patrick Day Party,** which was not until March of that year, I asked him, *"Was this to be my first, or second and last date with you"*? He laughed at my inquires, *"What do you mean by that"* he asked. I stated what I heard from other people, how he never dated any one more than twice. *"O that, don't worry, we will go* *out more than twice"*. My first date with John was bowling. We walked everywhere; he did not have a car, driver's license, or a *job*. He claimed to be an electrical contractor with his own business. Work was slow, so he was on *unemployment compensation*. This situation would change, faster than John thought, my father saw to that. As we continued to date, our second date was dinner at his home 405 W. Roselyn St. Phila. I met his family, mother, Katherine, sister Nancy Ann and brother Joe, his other sister Kathy Kasakowski was in CA with her husband Al and son Albert. After dinner we took the K bus over to the **CAMM shrine on Chelten Ave. for a novena to the Blessed Mother.** I knew than my parents, mom more than dad would like this nice Catholic man, even though he was

unemployed and never went into any of the US services, not because he was dodging the draft,

John was 4F. We dated for a while, and a class ring from North Catholic would seal our commitment until he could save for an engagement ring. He purchased the ring with his last unemployment check. I still have that little ¼ diamond; it will go to one of the Hopkins granddaughters some day when I join mom, dad, and John T. in the Lords mansion. John T. Hopkins and I were engaged in May of 1962 and our wedding set for Jan. 5, 1963. Early winter, before the wedding it was a bitter cold December day in1962 when, the front door of the office I worked at flew open, and in whizzed no other than Private Tom J. Z... My heart leaped and dropped at the same time. *"Hi"* he said, like I just saw him yesterday. *"I came to ask why you returned all my mail unopened letters for the last 3 years"*? I told him my tale of woe. *"Oh"* he said, *"That was over long ago, just after I enlisted"*. *"Let's go out tonight, I'll tell you all about it over dinner,"* he also stated to me *"I made a big mistake."* It was then I informed him of my upcoming wedding in two weeks. He actually got on his knees in front of me, and my three employers, and begged me not to go through with the wedding. I laughed so hard I almost chocked. He stated, *"If you go through with this marriage, I will reenlist in the Army again."* I told him, *"Tom, have a nice hitch"*. I often hear a song that Patsy Cline sings, that said it all in the lyrics, **"I got your picture, she's got you.**" well I had his Army ring, and so did she (the girl named Barbara).

He gave two rings to two girls, only one girl won. I was the loser. So, I thought at the time. I think about my situation with Tom, and if I had listened to the words in that song back in c.1959-1960 I would have given him up on the first fib. I don't think it ever got through Tom's head that **we** ended in 1960. My wedding day was perfect; John T. Hopkins and I were married and started a wonderful life together.

Tom called us, John, and I just two days ago, March 28, 2018, to ask when the book will be out? I asked him, if he would like to be taken out of it? Or change his name, "No," he said, "I did that a long time ago. I am who I am." I said, "one last chance befor the printed book will be published." Tom said he is ok with the story.

My story of first love now told.

After the death of my dearest John T. Hopkins, Tom Z... called, he had seen the death notice in the paper and asked me out again, I would have gone, just *to see what life had dealt him in the past 36 years*, but he was divorced from his first wife M, and not sure if he had remarried. I told him, I would not go out or date a devoiced man it is against my Catholic faith and my good judgement. Why was he always so persistent, or have a story to tell**? Was I the girl that got away?** At seventeen no one can say they know what love and commitment is. At that age the steps in our lives from childhood to young adulthood are just taking hold, with a long way to go, at least mine was. I am remarried since February 14, 2003 to a wonderful man; I danced with in high school (Cardinal Dougherty) when we were only juniors back in 1959. He was just a boy at the time, the one in a **Brown Suit**. John C. Lynch always seemed to be in the back ground of my adult life, as John T. Hopkins was during my high school days. As I mentioned before, at our ten-year reunion from CDHS I presented JC with a bottle of wine, we were both happily married and had children at that time. When our children began high school, they attended CDHS also. We the Hopkins and the "Lovely Lynch's" as JC likes to call his family, always seemed to connect in some way. We four were band parents and members of the CD mothers and fathers club. So as years past and reunions continued, I and John C. Lynch would volunteer to work on the reunion committee. On November 30, 1999, my husband John T. died. I found John gone (dead), when I returned home from my job at Conti Mortgage Co. I will tell you about our life together in a different chapter.

I continued to help on the reunions. On May 1, 2002 Janet E. Lynch passed away suddenly. On Sunday, July 14, 2002, John C., and I were reunited at the general reunion for CD alumni at the Sea Isle Yacht. With two deaths in common, and much loneness, and need for compassion and companionship, John and I connected by phone, July 28th, 2002. On the first call I received from John, it went like this, "*Hi, John C. Lynch from the Holy City of Cheltenham calling for Elaine*". I enjoyed hearing his voice, since we had played phone tag for two weeks. His first question to me in

July of 2002 was, *"What are you doing St. Patrick's Day, my church is having a St. Patty's party?* (I nearly dropped the receiver), now this date, if I accepted it, would not take place for eight months. Finally, while we were still connecting with each other John backed our first date up to the present time, and on August 2nd. 2002. Our second date would be dinner at the Glenside Pub, I was to meet him there 5:00 PM sharp, but before dinner he put me in his car and he took me to the **CAMM on Chelten Ave. to the *Shrine of the Blessed Mother for the Novena.*** This was as if I was back in 1961 all over again. I knew the relationship was more than

friends consoling one another. It was Heaven sent. With God in my life, I was always taken care of. We were engaged by September 2002, and married Friday, February 14, 2003. We danced to Nat King Cole's "That Sunday, that

Summer" How true to the song.

Was it too soon after John's wife Janet's death? Or did we move too fast on our first encounter? Everyone, my sons, his daughters told us to give it time. We did not listen we went down the church aisle as planned. Now December 2017, we are in our fifteenth year of happily married bliss and will celebrate our fifteenth anniversary on Feb. 14, 2018, which will be a small milestone for us (at our age of 75 years, we cherish each year as they pass). In 2003 we honeymooned in St. Lucia, time has passed, and we are working to keep the honeymoon fresh. All married people **must** work at it or it will not work for you, just a word to the wise. From time to time, Tom Z… would touch base with me, trying to get me to attend an old Germantown neighborhood reunion. When he called Dec. c2002 I again for a second time, informed him of my upcoming wedding this time to John C. Lynch. Tom asked if he and his wife Jul would be invited to the wedding. We, John C. Lynch, and I invited them; I wanted him to see **my life continued without him**. As my four sons John, Kevin, Stephen, and Michael walked me down the aisle of Presentation BVM Church the night of my wedding, the first persons I saw in the pew was Tom and his lovely wife. **I have**

been very happy and content with my entire life; I hope, and prayed Tom found peace and love with his lovely second wife. Tom was part of the story of my encounter with an infatuation of what I thought was first love. ***Beware of the first ONE***, it bites hard. It was November 2014, Tom checked in again with me. ***"Just friends he said"***, I hope he knows he was seventy-three years old then. Not seventeen It is Dec 11, 2017 now and Tom called today, we talked quite a while. After all these years, he finely asked, ***"How Barbara R and I ever got to meet each other***?" I told him it was "**God.**" It is the only explanation; God was always there for me. Tom and I were not meant to be. With a **tone** in his voice I never heard before. He said, "I am truly sorry." And for the first time in years I unequivocally, believed him. Age must do something to people, and God did   prevail.

How I cure a heartache

When your heart hurts, and no doctor can fix it. The hurt is not from sickness, but because a love is broken, love loss to a death, or the one you love pains it, with harsh words, that cut like a knife. How do you mend a broken heart? Drink take pills, some people do that, the heart never heals, and the brain dulls. I have had many heavy heartaches. As a small child when my world was turned upside down I thought it would never mend. When I was a love struck sixteen-year-old, as I stepped out of CD High School the last day, and when Dad left me on his birthday, no party, just his funeral, oh how my heart ached. Dad went so fast, I was not able to tell him I was sorry for things I thought he did, that made me angry. When Grandmom Weldon and Mom went home to the Lord, my heart had been marred. Then there was the night I found John T. Hopkins gone forever, I did not get the chance to tell him I was sorry for things I did that may have hurt him, he was gone, now in God's hands, all these episodes of pain leaves scars. People deal with it in many ways.

I just start to walk. It takes me on a path that has a long chain link fence. No matter when, I always find a path to a fence, as I walk, I run my index finger along the holes in the fence, at first it tickles, as I go further, my finger starts hurting more as I approach mid-way, when I come to the end of the fence. My whole hand is sore, with this new pain, the heartache has subsided. The scars remain, but the memories fade from the heart ache, but not my mind. I have found the walk in my life as I age, getting longer; I hope I can find a fence just as long to always ease the hearts pain. God knows what I do while walking along the fence, prayers always help.

I often use titles, or lyrics of songs that remind me of my heart. There is one that mentions "Be careful it's my heart" I wish I could say this to the one I love, before the pain begins. I found myself along the fence last night, Friday June 5, 2015. We, JC and I had some strong words. We did forgive all, but these are my inner thoughts I share with you on how I mend my heart ache.

MY BIG STEP DOWN FROM CARDINAL DOUGHERTY

September 1959, I approached my senior year at Cardinal Dougherty, I wanted to get as much as I could of this magnificent school. I remained in the glee club, studied as well as I could, while holding two jobs and helping mom with our home life. This year 1959-60 flew by. In English Lit I listened to the tape recording of Macbeth, as we read this requirement. When we were tested on it, I scored 100. The nun knew I did not cheat, because the girls that sat around my seat got 80's and 85's. I was in total shock myself, when she told me to stand up, and announced my mark. Not to brag, but I was the only senior that got 100 in the test. The year was ending too fast. Prom, Graduation practice at Convention Hall, Baccalaureate Mass. Finally, Saturday June 11, 1960 was graduation day. We had parties, went to parties, and totally enjoyed that weekend. On Monday June 13, 1960 we had to return our rented cap and gown. I arrived at school early to return the items. I entered the school for the first time thru the main doors. All visitors must enter through the front doors of the school (We students always had to go into school by the side doors.) It did not occur to me that I was a visitor. As I stood there in front of the auditorium and watched the once under classman, now the new seniors to be, walking around helping the nuns collect books etc. I wanted to help too, this was my home, my school for four years, but I was no longer a student there. I was just another visitor. I continued to stand in the main lobby, just by the front doors of this magnificent school. I could not move. I was frozen in time. It was as if my feet were glued to the floor. Ironically it was Sister Marie Lawrence an S.S.J. nun, who had taught me in my junior year Office Practice. She approached me, she saw my dismay. Sister said, *"Come on Elaine, I'll walk you out the door."* I was like a robot, I just moved along with her. The first day at CD flashed before me, it was as though it was just yesterday, now it was today, my last day at CD. We reached the open doors, it was as if I was in a daze, my emotions were out of control. This was my comfort zone for four years. It was my place of peace and solace. I had been safe here at Cardinal Dougherty High School. Where was I to go, what was I to do? Tears rolling down my face, I could not see clearly. Sister said *"Elaine; it's time for you to step forward now. Go out into the world and be as good as you were here at CD. Go on, go."* I took one step down off and on to the ground outside the front of Cardinal Dougherty High School, and that was it. I was now out on my own, to face a new world. It was one of my **biggest steps forward.** I had no idea what was ahead for me? Now here I am, telling you all about my wonderful life as A Slice of the PIE

I will continue with some more of the best part of the pie, and my life. Also, I hope you look to the two delicious recipes included in the story and the PIE. I will not be giving my siblings tales in order of birth, but in the order as things happened throughout my life with them.

THE   Bulova   WATCH
My   Godson   and   Brother   Dennis

Mother being the good catholic person she was, had this thing, that you had to go to confession every two weeks, whether you sinned or not. So, every other Saturday, all the little Py's, including my adult self, and those siblings who made their First Holy Communion, would have to do the march up to church by 4:00 PM. to tell our sins. Most of the time we made up sins, so now we sinned by telling a lie. Well this is my watch story. Denny my little four or five-year-old brother, not to be exact to his age, and Johnny Lewis were friends, and so was Mom with Kathleen Lewis, Johnny's mom. I think somewhere in line we were related or close enough to be so. One day Denny came home with the face of a beautiful Bulova watch. It was white gold, with diamonds on both sides of the face of the watch. There was no band, so you could not wear it. *"Denny,"* I asked, *where did you get this*? he said he found it. I had the watch Uncle John; my Godfather gave me when I graduated eight grade on my wrist. As I stated before, it was not very feminine. I ask Denny, If *I give you this watch, we can trade, and I will take that and get a band for it. OK,*" my little brother agreed. He was happy he had a watch to wear. I headed up 5th Street to BARR'S Jewelry store and purchased a Speidel watch band. The Bulova was a wind-up watch, it kept perfect time and it looked marvelous on my wrist. Time past and Mother was on her regular ritual about three weeks into my new watch. Before confession we always had to stop at Kathleen Lewis's house on the way to church. Mom would have her usual two highballs, (for you fancy drink people that would be a shot of whiskey & ginger ale over a glass of ice). This helped her to conjure up all her sins. The younger siblings would just eat some pretzels or chips and run outside to play while mother and I would sit in the Lewis's kitchen. I'd have a coke while just sitting there taking in weeks' worth of family and neighborhood gossip. Kathleen took notice to my watch that Saturday afternoon. She commented how nice it looked on my wrist. She stated she had one very similar to it, but she did not wear it anymore. It was her grandmothers, then her mothers, and she received the watch at her graduation from high school over 19 years ago. It was a family heirloom passed on from generation to generation. With that statement, I asked a dreaded question, "Where *is your watch now Kathleen?*" She said, *"Up in the jewelry box in my bed room, the band broke, and it is just the face of the watch",* well my face turned flush color, and I asked her, if she didn't mind showing me her watch. While mother was meditating over her second highball, she missed my conversation with Mrs. Lewis. Kathleen arrived back in the kitchen, and stated *the watch was missing.* I gently removed her watch from my wrist. *"Here Kathleen"* I said. *"This is your watch",* I proceeded to tell the story that Denny told me about finding it, and how I traded my watch for this one. Kathleen informed me her son Johnny and Denny were playing in her home and must have gotten into her bed room and took the piece of jewelry from the box. I apologized, for my brother and Johnny's antics and was glad it fell into my hands. I said, "little kids don't realize values, they must have thought it was broken, and just watched time go by on it while playing in your room." I got up, and started out to find Denny, so I could retrieve my old watch he had been wearing. Mrs. Lewis stopped me *"no!"* She said "I want you to keep it. Consider it a late graduation gift to you. I have not used it in years;

you wear it well and remember the age of it". Today as I write the Dennis story, this watch I have is over 115 years old and still ticking. I had it overhauled by Bulova, for my second wedding over 15 years ago. I only wear it on dressy occasions. My granddaughter Laura Hopkins Been has picked it to be part of my legacy to her. All seven of my Hopkins granddaughters have chosen my Hopkins jewelry as my last gifts to them. I have instructed them, that they come, and take what they chose, along with the crystal goblet I purchased for them to toast to me, when I am no longer on this earth. We all know we cannot take it with us. *Cheers to you girls. My Hopkins granddaughters, Jessica, Brittney, Jackie, Laura, Katie, Jenna, Izabella, Love Grandmom Elaine.*

Jumping ahead, Summer of 2014 I must write this now while it is fresh on my mind. My 71st summer began on June 21, 2014, but our Cheltenham Pool (Conklin) opened Saturday June 14th. It was a clear sunny day the temps were in the middle to high 70's. Just to say we did it, we went on opening day. The pool was a little brisk for us old folks to venture into the water. John and I made the best of this summer. In June we took four of the

Hurst (our grandchildren Brigid, Henry, Moira and Sinead to N. Wildwood, NJ) for four days. Upon returning on Thursday of that week we again enjoyed our Township pool. On July 18th we were invited to use a neighbor's seashore cottage for that weekend, John and I attended the Cardinal Dougherty Soar at the Shore, Saturday July 19, 2014 the general reunion where JC and I met again twelve years ago, only it was on a Sunday July 14, 2002 held at the Sea Isle Yacht Club. It is now held in North Wildwood. We usually ride our bikes to the event from wherever we are staying, this year we biked from Maple Ave. (Rio Grande area) to North Wildwood, 3rd and New Jersey Avenues. This was a task to be proud of. We returned home on the 20th, only to find out we could have stayed in the cottage all week. Upon our return we continued spending our lazy dog days of summer at the neighborhood pool, thru the month of July. With August moon approaching, every chance we got we were at the pool. August 13, 2014, back to N. Wildwood, NJ for the PY family yearly gathering, we took Brigid, my Hurst granddaughter, along, so she could see, and share time with my large family. I let her stay up late, since September was approaching, and school would soon start. She hung with me and all the adults, Thursday night we played 31, a card game, until two AM. I think, her Pop-Pop was a little angry to say the least, for me keeping her out so late. We were just outside our room #110, but you know Pop pops. Moving right along, the 3rd week in August we spent a wonderful weekend in Toms River NJ, with our dear friends the Corkery's. They have a lovely home on a lagoon. Need I say more? Well, yes, driving home, we missed a turn and we ended up (UP) in North Jersey toward Trenton. Oh well, it was a beautiful Sunday, and the roads were not crowded, so we just mapped our way back to the old Tacony Palmyra Bridge, getting home too late to go to the Pool. Labor Day weekend approached early that year, August 29th to Sept. 1st we must have been very popular because we had four places to visit over that weekend. Every year there is a 3-day event at the Cannstatter German Club, located on Academy Rd. in Northeast Philadelphia. The event   starts on the Saturday of Labor Day weekend and goes to late Monday evening. John and I usually go on Sunday, but due to our busy calender that weekend we decided to do Saturday. The. venue is German food, and German bands they play wonderful music to waltz to, along with the Chicken Dance, the whole crowd loves it. The drink of the day is Warsteiner Beer for the real German beer drinkers. My all Irish husband John joins the German beer drinkers. (When in Germany...you know the rest). I will have my sweet Amaretto, or a Malibu with Coca Cola. The bratwurst platter, with German potato salad is our favorite. I am getting hungry just typing about it. On this busy weekend, my sister Patty invited us to her pool to swim, and dinner at her home after the swim for Sunday. My son Stephen and wife Peggy Hopkins extended an invite to his home for a swim and a cookout, on Sunday also. Monday our pool would close for the summer, we plan to be there for the final day. Saturday, we slept in, since we had an unexpected trip on Friday to Doylestown Hospital to pick up Michael my youngest son, who had an emergency hernia operation, and being the good Samaritans, we are known to be, we volunteered to drive him from the hospital to Long Port, NJ where his little family had been spending the end of the summer in their home by the Atlantic Ocean. The New Jersey shore is last place to be driving to on the last holiday weekend of the summer. Family love always prevails. Finally, John and I arrived home quite late from this fast trip to the sea shore, due to missing a left turn out of Margate, NJ trying to get on the

Garden State Parkway northbound. We ended up in a DUI check point, and with the luck of the Irish, the Great Lynch was one of the drivers that was pulled out of line to be checked. Can you imagine? "The Great Lynch, police officer" being pulled over by no other than another police officer? Once the officer saw John was a former Marine, all went well. The officer sent us on our way. Halfway home we gassed up and had a late-night Milk Shake, to cool our jets. Sunday, we went to 8:30 Mass and after a mid AM breakfast, up to Steve's to swim, saw some of my Hopkins grandchildren and great grandchildren. We left when the rain started. On the way home, we pull into Patty's to have one last cocktail for the summer. The finest day of the whole 2014 summer, Mass at St. Joseph's Church. By 12 noon I had two umbrellas staked out at the Cheltenham pool. We expected John's cousin Andy Farley and his family to arrive, we would need two to shade the hot sun. The sky was blue, the sun shining bright, not a cloud in the sky, and it was tipping 90 degrees just past noon. What more could one expect, well I got the biggest surprise in many years. I was determined that this day could not end, sort of like my last day as a child on 28th Street. It was too perfect, family, friends what more could anyone want. There I was in the pool for every adult swim. At the top of each hour the life guard would blew the whistle for all children to vacate the pool, and let the adults have fifteen minutes of peaceful pool time to themselves. The last whistle sounded to allow the children back in, I remained in the pool just enjoying this last day of our swimming. It was fifteen past four o'clock, children, adults, all just jumping, yelling, splashing, it was like deja vu for me in those last few minutes. I was back in time, the summer of 1948 at the Whittier Pool and playground. A flash of my past was with me in the present. It did not matter if my hair got wet, or I was kicked by a passing swimmer or splashed in the eyes; it was that moment that brought me back to my first memories and beginning steps as a PY. Today can never be repeated, I will lock it in my heart, and just remember.

We would be heading to North Carolina on September 4th and then a 4 day stop in, Virginia Beach, VA on Sept. 8th to follow a fall summer. We had an unexpected trip to the wonderful City of St. Augustine, FL in October for nine days, another part of geography and history I missed in my youth. So much to see. We journeyed home to PA, to settle in for the rest of the seasons, looking forward to snow birding in the winter months in the Condo on the beautiful Myakka River, in Port Charlotte, FL, and summers at Cheltenham pool.

Sibling-Stories

My brothers and sisters have many PY stories to tell of their own. I will write a few episodes that happened during our life as Py's on Second Street that I like to share. These true tales are presented not in birth order, just as I think of everyone. **The Bulova Watch story was Denny's caper. My godson has come a long way since that five-year-old little boy**. He is now a grandfather, and his youngest daughter Michele will be married to Jeffrey Stine, on Halloween October 31, 2015. The wedding will be a Formal Dress Gala Ball. It will be wonderful to see all my brothers and sisters, dressed to kill, (sort of speak) in formal attire.

The last time we did a complete Py family photo was many years ago on July 6th, 1974, when Joe and Ruth were married. Mom, Dad, Joe the groom and the rest of us siblings are featured in this photo, one that cannot be repeated. Four of our Pie in this photo have gone home to be with our God in Heaven. Dad, Jan. 26, 1976, Mom, June

11, 1995, our sister Marian, Sept. 1, 2017, and brother Bill, Jan. 11, 2018.

Py Family July 6, 1974

The Little King – Joseph Py US Navy, Senior Chief Petty Officer, E8

My curly hair brother Joe's best friend, Joe Hettler's dad had a bakery in our Philadelphia neighborhood when we were growing up. The two Joe's would do odd jobs for Mr. Hettler the baker. My brother chose to go to Mercy Technical School for high school, he took up baking. Mr. Hettler let

Joe Py work at the bakery. As the neighborhood started to change, the baker moved his business and family to Warminster, PA. While my brother was still in school, he continued to travel to the new bakery located on Street Rd. near Davisville Rd. as a part time worker. Now Joe was just sixteen and had a junior driver's license. This meant he could not be driving without a licensed driver along with him between ten PM and seven AM. One day Joe was driving at five AM, on his way to the bakery. As he drove across Cheltenham Ave. he was stopped by one of the township police officers, who asked why he was out so early in the morning, Joe explained he worked in a bakery. The officer told my brother he would need a letter from his employer stating his hours of work. He was to carry this letter along with his driver's license while driving in the early morning hours. All was well; Joe had the letter and did not have any problems. Now Mr. Hettler had a lot of property and he needed fertilizer for his lawn. We had a neighbor, Ed Cassel who owned horses, he kept them in the back of his property on Mentor Street, so Joe told Mr. Hettler he would bring him some fresh manure on his next work day. Joe got five four-gallon wooden barrels, filled them with the horse shit and started up toward Cheltenham

Avenue. As he crossed from the Philadelphia County into Cheltenham Township, Montgomery County, heading to Bucks County, he was pulled over by two Cheltenham Township officers. One of the officers asked, "Why are you out so early on a junior license.? Joe presented his letter. The officer noticed the car was sagging in the rear, so he asked Joe "What's in the trunk." My brother replied, "Nothing but a bunch of shit sir." The officer shouted at Joe ("Don't get wise with me young man groaned the officer, "Now what is in the trunk?" Joe again stated "SHIT". "Get out of the car and open the trunk," barked the officer. Joe did as requested. Now it was 5:00 AM and still dark. The police man grabbed a crow bar, and pried open one of the barrels, the cop proceeded to push his hand and arm deep into the barrel, and needless to say, a photo would have said it all. "WELL" the other officer stated, "The boy told you what was in the trunk, nothing but a bunch of shit." They sent him packing and told him not to come by this way again.

Ed Cassel also owned an oil delivery business; he always pulled his truck up to 4722 N. 2nd. Street to fill our oil tank with oil. Mom never had any money to pay Ed, but we always had oil and the old steam heat kept coming through those old radiators to keep us warm in the cold of winter. When mother died, I wanted to pay Ed his bill of fare, he would not hear of it. Today, as I have long since moved on in life, I encountered Ed Cassel again; he was the Chief of Cheltenham Auxiliary Police. When I see him, we remember days of old and have many good laughs. Ed passed on Nov. 21, 2016. I will always remember his generosity to our Py family.

Joe Py could, and should write a book of his own, but he is a cook at National Living History Events Rendezvous.

Giada Italy—A truth that happened to Joe during his twenty-four years in the US Navy.

The one I chose to tell is a tale of a full circle. As in the beginning I told of Dad being in Italy during the Second World War. He and George his Captain would go to a little bakery for fresh bread in Giada, while they waited for the dough to rise, and finish baking, they would distribute candy bars to the proprietor's children. The owner would take photos of the GI's on their jeeps, and with his children. He had about six kids. One boy about nine was the favorite son, the dad would say, "My boy will own this place someday."

Joe's ship was anchored at a port in Italy. Joe and some of his ship mates were on a liberty call in the same area where the old bakery was. Dad had died in 1976; he never knew Joe would be in Italy. Joe never heard dad's candy bar distribution story. One afternoon he and some of his mates enter a bar for a cold beer. The owner greeted the sailors, and questioned their names, and origin. My brother introduced himself as PY, the bar keeper asked, "was your father in the Second World War"? Joe answered "yes", now the owner requested Joe to follow him, as they walked, Joe was informed that the bar had been a bakery back in the 1940's. By now Joe was standing in front of a large cork bulletin board with photos plastered all over it. There were many US Service members pictures on the board. The gentlemen pointed to a photo of Dad and George on an Army Jeep, and asked is this your dad? This was probably the first time my brother Joe was speechless. Yes, it was our Dad. Joe was informed the owner of the bar, was the boy that our father gave the chocolate bar to. GI's were noted for distributing their rations to the children around the town, but who would have thought, years later, much after World War II ended, that this adult would still remember his childhood and the good deed of our Dad, and even his name, Bill Py

My Brother Bill
US Navy Retired, Master Chief Petty Officer Bus Boy and Home

Billy was like me, the second of ten, he had to help support our family. During his years at Cardinal Dougherty High School, class of 1963, he worked for Linton's Restaurant's (they owned a chain of them throughout the city of Philadelphia) Bill was a busboy. He too would turn most of his earnings over to Mom; she would than purchase PTC tokens for Bill to get to and from work. She kept them in a clear crystal glass in the china cabinet. (Surprised she still had crystal in c.1962-63). Dad's work took him into New Jersey a lot when he was in Local 19. (Dad even did welding on the tops of the Spinnakers High Rise Apartment Buildings constructed in 1972, they are the twin buildings located at the beach front in Sea Isle City, they are now expensive condominiums); dad's job sites moved around a lot, after he no longer worked at the Carrier Building, just around the corner. When one was a union member they never knew where a new bid would be situated. My mom also purchased bridge tokens for dad to get to NJ. each day, Dad and Bill would grab their (tokens) from the glass in the cabinet for the trips to and from work. Off they went. Bill had been transferred to the Linton's in the Kingsessing area to fill in for vacations. When his shift was over, one of the bosses would drop him off at City Hall (Old Billy Penn's located on the North Broad Street side of Market Street, so Bill could board the C bus north, or take the subway. This one-day Bill chose the C Bus, upon entering the bus, and giving the driver his fare, the man stated, "this is a bridge token I can't except this son," no bus for Bill, no money for a phone call, or to ride the bus, he had grabbed one of Dads bridge tokens rather than a PTC one. My brother walked from Willy Penn's statue at Broad and Market St, to 2nd and Wyoming Ave. Good boy, busser, Navy man, my brother Bill.

Billy was cut out early to be a sailor c.1955, Dad, Uncle John, my brother Bill would go deep sea fishing it was during the time the Catholic Church kept the NO MEAT on Friday law. They would bring home a multitude of different kind of fish: Blue Fish Mackerel, and Porgies. Dad would scale all the fish keep plenty for us and put the rest out on the pavement and call all the neighbors to come get their free fresh fish. Try saying that fast. I called it the three F's. Bill was fascinated by the ocean, the fish, and the ships he saw as a boy while catching the Friday's meal.

Bill and Carol raised four daughters, Karen, Sandra, Nichole, and Dannielle. The family moved with him when he was transferred from duty station to duty station. Finally, when he retired they purchased their third home, of many, on the 6000 block of N. Fairhill St., Philadelphia, PA. He waited for his first two daughters Karen and Sandy to graduate Olney High School. Bill and Carol then purchased a brand-new home located at 501 Franklin Ave., Cheltenham, PA. He was smart, after staying there until the two younger girls Nichole and Daniel graduated Cheltenham High School, he then claimed the Cheltenham taxes were too high, (and they are, a single home ia about $6,750.00 I know because we pay ours). Bill & Carole moved to the 9100 block of Haldeman Ave. Phila. PA. During all the moves, Sandy Py had married Jose Rodriguez, Bill and Carol became grandparents to her three children, Willie Py, Samantha, and Joey Rodriguez after they were in the home in Philadelphia, my niece Sandy found her husband dead about March 1998 of a brain bleed, an aneurysm and ten months later, November 30, 1998 Sandy, my brothers second daughter joined her husband Jose in Heaven, she died from untreatable breast cancer. The couple left behind three children of a tender age. Bill had been thinking of retiring from the US Postal Service after 20 some years of service, at sixty-two, he and his wife Carol planned to do some traveling; just for pleasure, to see the rest of the world as civilians. Well they traveled all right, to preschools, grade schools, and high school while struggling to raise their three grandchildren. During this time, there was a popular ABC-TV reality show "Extreme Makeover—Home Edition that appeared once a week on Sunday evening at eight o'clock. It starred Ty Pennington. You remember (MOVE THAT BUS) Hey there's that word **bus** again, how ironic. The show always had a theme. There was one for Grand Parents raising grandchildren. A friend of Karen's named (John) told his mom about Bill and Carol raising their grandchildren. John's mom entered Bill and Carol Py into the contest. **News flash on KYW's David Madden show**, stated c. March 2006 "Extreme Makeover—Home Edition" has taken over a street in Northeast Philadelphia where a split-level home will be torn down and rebuilt in less than a week while the resident's vacation in Puerto Rico. He stated, "Bill and Carol Py looked forward to retirement in their home on Haldeman Avenue until fate stepped in: Their daughter and her husband tragically passed away and left three kids: A neighbor's daughter, stated to ABC "They're really good people. they're kind. They helped me out when I was growing up and helped my family out". Well it was my Brother Bill Py's family and home he was commenting about. Bill got a chance to board that **bus**, without a token (Ty's bus). My brother's family had a new home. We were there, all nine of us Py's, and extended family and friends, while Bill, Carol and the three grandchildren vacationed in Puerto Rico We were part of the TV production, we watched the home be demolished, and stayed night and day around the clock for seven days while a new home was constructed on the old site. We were treated like royalty. No one from the Py family should have to lift a hand. Although a lot of our sons and daughters jumped in to help. It poured rain for three days straight during the rebuild. No one would leave, only to go home to sleep, or work, and then back on the site. On the seventh day, like in the Old Testament, God rested. The builders did too. When the huge coach bus was parked outside Bill's new home on the seventh day, we all rested and waited in anticipation, waiting for the white limo to arrive. Late afternoon the vehicle turned slowly onto Haldeman Ave. The crowd who aligned the street for about a 1/2-mile-long began to cheer; Bill Py and family arrived, our family was escorted from the limo, and stood in front of the bus. The chant began, "Move That Bus", it was repeated over and over. Slowly the engine of the bus started, and the bus began to move like a turtle, anticipation surrounded the entire are. In place of the large bus, was a beautiful new two-story state of the art large home. One well deserved by my brother Bill and his family. At least six or seven years have passed, and Bill, Carol and the children moved to Florida for health reasons. He must have missed Ty's bus so much after he moved to Florida; he purchased a forty-eight-foot Coach Bus for travel. Happy Motoring Bill you deserve it. Now as I sit here Jan. 27, 2018, with tears streaming down my face, and my heart heavy with pain, I think of the last time I saw and spoke to my baby brother. I visited him in a rehab center in Orlando FL on Dec. 30, 2017. I see a frail man in and out of consciousness lying in his hospital bed. I asked, "Bill do you know me?" he mumbled low but clear, "big sister". I then said "would you like to pray with us? (me, my husband John, and his wife Carol) Bill shook his head yes. I held his cold hands, and said the Act of Contrition with him, as his six-year-old great grandson Liam stood at the foot of his bed. I told Bill, "it is OK to go, God is waiting." He squeezed my hand. We started to leave, John handed the boy (Liam) a $5.00 bill, for being so very good during our visit, I commented "five bucks, when great grand pop and I were kids, we thought it great to get a nickel" everyone laughed even my brother Bill. It was the last laugh, (his) On Jan. 11, 2018 by phone I prayed in his ear as the Angles came to escort him home to Heaven. When Carole and his daughter shut the phone off, he smiled, closed his eyes and went home to God.

The next time I saw Bill, he was in his dress blue Navy uniform, it was Jan. 17, 2018 when he was laid to rest in a navy-blue coffin at the funeral home in Orlando FL. After his Catholic service with Father Jim, the family and friends were asked to approach the casket for the last farewell, I looked to the rear of the room, and saw Jack Rowan our first friend in the new home when they were 4 yrs. old and I was 7. I took Jack by the hand, and we walked together as we did the three of us so many times before, we knelt in front of my brothers place of rest, then Jack and I touched Bills cold hands, I said, "Jack we said hello together 67 years ago, it is now time for you, Bill and I to say Good Bye," we did. As we knelt at Bills casket, Jack and I wept together as we use to laugh together with a much livelier Bill. We looked at each other with tears falling from our eyes, and just stood up, turned our backs on Bill and walked out of the funeral home.

Tears for the years we the Py family shared together with Bill, will still flow down when we reminisce of happier times, we can cherish the memories of years past forever.

My baby brother Bill Py Nov. 5, 1945-Jan 11, 2018. He will never be forgotten. He will be remembered by all, as a **giver** and **never a taker. The only things he ever took, were other people's problems, and tried to help us all**.

Thank you, brother Bill. Keep a Heavenly eye on us. Love big sis, Elaine.

My dearest Sister Patty, my roommate.

It was the summer of 1959 upon my return from the Girl Scout trip to Colorado Springs, I found the day-bed that I slept on for years in our front bed room had been moved to the living room. (Not to mention I kept my private diary under the mattress of that bed). All my thoughts and secrets had been read by all. We did not have much privacy on Second Street. Mom put me in their back bedroom with my sister Patty. Me being the oldest, and Patty the next oldest girl in our Pie Shell, (6 years younger) we were lucky to get to share a bed room to ourselves. Mom and Dad decided to give up their room and move downstairs to a sofa bed. Our sister Marie, just a year younger than Patty, now shared the front room with the younger three girls, Marian, Kathleen (Pete) and the new baby Jeannie. The four boys Bill, Joe Rich, and Denny were stacked in bunk beds in the middle bed room. My parents did the best they could within the space they had. I was pleased to finally have some privacy. Our back bedroom was always very cold in the winter, and extremely hot in the summer. No matter what the conditions were, we enjoyed our new space. I, being the oldest girl, and a big sister, when it came time for Pat to learn about life, and the birds, and the bees, I took it upon myself at age eighteen to tell her what Mother never could bring herself to tell any of us girls. Pat and I shared many stories while we bunked together. At age twenty I was to marry John Hopkins and begin a new life away from Second Street.

One mid-December night in 1965, very close to the Christmas holidays, the phone in our home on Tampa Street rang. When I picked it up; it was Mother, I could tell by her voice she was very upset, she could hardly get out the words. "Patty is pregnant" she blurted in my ear. I was pregnant to have my third baby, who was due in April of 1966. I sat there and just looked into the receiver of the phone; I could hear her from the distance "Did you hear me?" I started to speak, "Mom, how could this happen? I told Pat the things you should have told us when we were becoming young ladies" I said. "Well it did" mother stated, in a much louder voice. I asked, "when is this baby to be born"? "Oh, I'm not sure, sometime in March the doctor told us" she rattled on. My mind was working overtime, I did not know what else to say, but Mother did. She screamed, "I' am not raising grandchildren; I raised ten children of my own". (Mother had been back working by then; my parents needed all the financial help they could get). I was informed by mom that Pat would go to St. Vincent's home for girls when the baby was due. The baby would be delivered sometime in March. This home/hospital for girls was run by Catholic Charities and the nuns. Then mom hit me with the bomb, the baby would be taken from my sixteen-year-old sister immediately after giving birth, and adopted out, to a nice Catholic family who were on the adoption waiting list, and that was that. I was shaken by now. I thought, we were a nice Catholic family, who took care of their own. A family member being raised by strangers, how can this be happening? My sister Pat had no say, about if she wanted to keep the baby, just as I had no say back in 1949, about not wanting to move. Many thoughts were flashing before me; maybe we (John and I could take this new life.) In 1965 John Hopkins's income was minimal. This thought left quickly. My husband John and I had two young son's ages one and two, and the third son of four would be born in April 1966. I could not ask my husband to take on another baby around the same time ours would be entering the world. Since mother had just found out about the pregnancy maybe as time went on she would change her mind, and somehow, we could keep this new life in our family, after all it would be a PY. It had been one of the nuns in Cardinal Dougherty High School that questioned my sister about her weight gain and came right out and asked if she was in a family way. Pat was afraid and relieved at the same time. I did not understand why Pat could not tell me, I guess she thought I would not be able to help her unburden this situation, so she kept this problem bottled up inside for about five months. She was expelled from school as soon as the nuns found out, and so was her boyfriend a senior in CDHS at the time. (Nowadays if a girl is pregnant they leave school and return after the birth of the baby, they even bring the child to their graduation) but this was not the way schools were run back in the 60's, at least not in a Catholic high school. Since the burden was lifted and Pat's secret was out, she must have relaxed, or panicked whichever it was, Pat went into early labor and a baby girl was born premature on January 3, 1966. She was immediately whisked away; Patty was unable to see, or even name the baby she gave life to. When Pat arrived home, she was unable to return to school, she had to go out into the work force and begin to help support the rest of our family. Not to mention she and the boy, were forbidden to see each other ever again. Both set of parents agreed on that, but not on whose fault any of this was, the parents of the father of the baby put all the shame on Pat. Time passed on, as it does, "The time and tide waits for no one", and somehow during this interval love bloomed again between Pat and the father of that little baby girl. A big church wedding was planned. After the marriage, the boy's mother wanted to go to the adoption agency and whisk that little two-year girl away from her loving parents. We all, (my mother, Pat, her husband, and I) said "NO" and that was that. In due time Patty and her husband had two loving sons, George, and Patrick. Pat and her husband even raised our niece Vicky Py, from age one and a half or two years old. There were times on Jan. 3rd I would call Pat and say, "do you know what today is", and as if she could ever forget, she would answer in a solemn voice "Yes". Over the years I would often ask Patty did she ever want to locate that girl. "NO" was always the answer. Was it the fear of the unknown, or just the fact that she was trying to forget what happened when she was just a young girl herself, caught in an unsolvable situation? I often said to Pat, "What would you do if that knock came on the door, and it was your own daughter asking, "Are you my mother"? Pat would always say, "It won't happen, and if it does, I will not open the door. "About four and a half years ago c.2013, (longer than that now 2018) I was driving to the store, and my cell phone rang, I pulled the car to a stop, and answered the call. It was Patty; she said, "my worst nightmare has come alive." Not being ready, (as I was not ready for mother's call back in 1965) but the sound of Pat's voice had fear in it as she spoke, the same fear my mon's voice had that December night. "My daughter is trying to locate me" stated Pat. I again just sat there looking into the cell phone. What was I to say? "I told you so", No, I just asked "what are you going to do?" Pat was not ready for what was forthcoming. She had a lot to think about, I did not advise either way, although I was hoping beyond hope that she would not let this little girl (now a woman of 45 years old) go again. In 1966 Pat was under our mother's control. Now Patty was in control. One thing happened over 20 some years ago, I did not mention, Pat's husband the, father of her three children left her for another woman over 14 years into their happy marriage. Sometimes I wonder, how long does love last? Not to be the blame for the divorce, it was about that time, Pat told her two sons the story of how their father, and she had a baby when they were just young teenagers, and that her sons had a biological sister somewhere in the world. Now that sister was within 40 miles of all their world and lives. Tara is her name and she had been trying to locate her birth parents and family since she was a young girl. Pat finally opened that door in response to a letter from her daughter. She told her sons of their sister trying to reach out. Everyone even the fraternal grandmother welcomed the news, (our mother will meet her granddaughter Tara in heaven someday). Tara is still trying to reach out to her father, he never told his new wife of the teenage trauma he, and his first wife Pat had gone through over 53 years ago. He also must still have that fear. Maybe someday Tara will get to know her biological father as she has come to know and love her mother, and brothers. Tara has two wonderful children a daughter Jena a 2018 collage grad and, a son David about 13 or 14). Tara is the reason for this part of the PIE, and Patty's story. She wants her birth story told. Tara was always part of the Py family, but never knew why she was given up for adoption. She has shared the love of her wonderful adopting parents and a brother. Her mother died when she was a young girl and the search for her birth mother has now come to an end, but the love between them is growing stronger all the time. My sixteen-year-old sister would not have found the love they are bound together with now, back when she was not quite an adult c.1966. All knocks should be answered in due time. Love knocked when it was needed by both. This was just the beginning of Patty's and Tara's new-found family and more members added to our PIE.

Marie, my second sister, how's that old fable go "New house new baby"

It sure held true for the Py family. My second sister, Marie, a June baby, was brought to our home on Second Street after mom had given birth to her on June 12, 1950 in Roxborough Memorial Hospital. Was that a coincidence or what? My sister Pat and Marie lived on Second Street for just over seventeen years   Marie and Patty were as close in age as they are very close and loving sisters to each other to this day. They were what are called Irish twins. The two girls did a lot together. As they reached high school, they would go to the roller skating rink; that and the movies were the most popular places to be. Marie met her husband at the rink. Oh, John was her boyfriend then. I was long gone since 1963, my brother Bill went in the Navy c1965, and Patty had joined the workforce, Marie was moved into being the chief cook and bottle washer at our house. (This is the truth). I am remembering the Italian family who moved into 4724 right next door to our home. The family consisted of, Mother (Nina) Father (Jack) the old grandmother, two adult sons and, two younger daughters. Both parents, and older sons worked. The older girl Antoinette, just thirteen at the time, went to school, came home, and prepared an entire dinner, from soup to nuts for her family. I could not have fantasied this. Our Mother was a stay at home mom, who cooked our meals every evening and was still raising younger children. I never thought anyone of my sisters would be doing what Antoinette had to do. Well in due time it happened, Mom had to work, I am not sure just what position dad was in at that time c1966. He may have been flat on his back, out of work, or working out of town? Nevertheless, the homemaking burden was placed on my sister Marie. She would come right home after school, and start cleaning up, and preparing the dinner for ten family members still living on Second St. Some of our siblings were still in the lower grades, so she had to keep an eye on them in between watching the stove. I want to say Marie was "sixteen going on seventeen"? Again, like in the song from a movie "The Sound of Music". Marie was not hearing music notes. She may have been thinking wedding bells? I want to think that my parents did not realize the burden they placed on my young sister. There were times she could not even go to the skating rink with her boyfriend. Finally, Mer eloped with John. Since she was given the job as homemaker, big sister (mother) to her siblings, she may as well have her own family. Marie and her husband John have three loveable children, Michele, Colleen, and Tim. They have given her two granddaughters and four grandsons. She is a wonderful wife, mother, and grandmother. Mer, as I call her is married forty-eight or forty-nine years to the boy from the roller rink. I must say Joe Py took up baking in school, but my sister Marie is the Baker of Bakers, and the meals she whips up are delicious. (If she hadn't left home), and did all she does now, and still works a full-time job as an underwriter for an insurance company, (no one else would have ever left the Second Street home, because my second sister, Mer certainly is a chief cook, and more.) Marie loves to tell jokes, and make people laugh, but never ask her for salt, you may just get a handful. Ha! This is a family joke. I did ask her just yesterday (Christmas Eve, 2017 to pass it to me, with a laugh, she did).

Flash back (Last night May 27, 2015,) I watched a classic film featured in 1969 on TCM. It was "Goodbye Mr. Chips." Peter O'Toole sang a beautiful song. Its title is "Where did my childhood go" "When did the magic end", What a heartfelt song, just listening to the lyrics brought tears to my eyes, it makes me think about all the Py children and where did our childhood go? I am sure my younger siblings considered Mer their little mom. Love you Mer.

Well it's getting late, and I don't mean by the clock. I am now seventy-five. I started this memoir just before I would have been seventy. I never thought of it being more than a short story of my family and our lives. It looks to me, that I have a novel in process. It puts a whole new spin on how I want this story to continue, and of course end. I have two sisters left to interject. Once again, my brother Richard is lost, I must write his story over since I lost it and him. So, Elaine let's get started. It is May 30, 2015 and it's fitting I introduce you to my **third sister Marian,** especially today. We sometimes call her Mammenuch. I know there is no such name as Mammenuch; I see the red line telling me I have yet again misspelled something. No, now that I look at the color of the line it is not **red**, it is **pink**. Is Pink Marians favorite color? We shall see. Trying to give you a photo image of Marian, well did you ever watch "Married with Children"? It was a TV series about a married couple with children. The mother's name in the show was "Peg Bundy". She had reddish hair and wore a lot of "leopard" colored style clothing, ah, now you know who she is. Well my sister Marian reminds me of Peg. When her hair was fuller than now, it also was red or medium auburn. Mar as we sometime call her, along with the other long name, is one special person, giddy, yes, Oh, and poetry, she has the gift to be able to write poems. She could have written for Hallmark Card Company. I wish I could compose like Marian does. She worked for Hanna's Auto Body and Fender in the Tacony section of Philadelphia as an automobile paint finisher. All the delicate details were her forte. Remember Ed Cassel, the person in my Brother Joe's tale about the horse manure? Ed owned a home oil business. His oil truck had to be refinished. He being friends with Marian and her husband Chuckie, Ed asked could they help him with a design logo for his oil business. Well since his name was Cassel, they painted the rear of the oil truck in a magical Castle. This truck made a hit and so did Mar and Chuck. The truck is long gone, but the photos and the memory linger on. When she was a little girl she had long reddish curly hair, a beautiful child. I lost track of her as a child after I was married. But some of the stories she could tell will send you into a whirl-wind. One time, when Dad had a car, he would drive the younger teens, Marian thirteen, and Jeanie, ten or near eleven years old to church on Sunday. He would drop them off, and go off, who knew where? Incarnation Church chimes would ring out, calling all to church, not dad, he would just wait for the girls outside the church. This one very windy Sunday, as Marian and Jeanie, came running to the car, Jeanie dropped a napkin, and it started to blow down Lindly Avenue, toward 5th street. Now this was not a tissue type napkin, it was a sanitary one that dropped out from under her. This thing maturity was very new to her; I was not around to explain the process to Jeanie, and I guess Mom forgot again, or eliminated the facts as usual. Well as the wind took it sailing, Marian started to chase after it. She kept running after it. Dad blowing the car horn and waiving to her to get the heck in the car, she paid no heed. She chased it until she snatched it from the pavement, and then returned to dad in the car. "OK kid" Dad blurted out, "Now just what are you going to do with that used item"? Poor Marian didn't want anyone to see this embarrassing item which would also embarrass her kid sister. Mar could find more drama than the queen herself.   Marian   was one of the youngest sisters to leave home. She didn't just leave home she left Pennsylvania, and went to California, she was just about fifteen. No one could tie her down; she knew what, and who she wanted. Her boyfriend Chuck was in the US Navy, and was stationed in CA, so she stationed herself there too. When they returned home to PA, Chuck asked dad for Maid Marian's hand in marriage. Dad and Mom went thru the roof. *NO*, was their answer. *"You two are too young, the marriage will not last, there's not going to be a marriage.* Well, like when she took off to CA, they took off to Yearkey's, a Justice of the Peace out in Upper Darby, PA.   After the ceremony, Marian called home to tell my parents of the nuptials, and she wanted to stop by and show mom her dress, and mend fences. When they arrived by car to the Second Street home, Dad was waiting on the front porch. He had a bucket of not confetti, not rice; but threw a bucket of water at them, and said, *"There now I blessed your marriage"*. Shame on dad, poor Marian just wanted his approval.

Eventually Dad and Mom accepted the marriage. Now Chuckie and Marian are married for forty-eight years or more; they have two sons, and a daughter. Marian is a grandmom and great grandmother. May 30, 2015, Marian, her children, husband, and all the Py family along with, I hope, two hundred or more relatives and other people will be wearing **PINK, *her favorite color*** showing our support and helping Marian's fight against cancer. Our youngest sister Jeanie came up with the plan to raise money to help defray the cost for the cure, not covered by insurance. Sisters helping Sisters. Mom, and dad we wish you could be here in person to cheer Mar on. It is supposed to be a very hot day, dad; maybe we could use that bucket of water. I must state, we had a five-minute rain shower that Saturday, our parents must have shed tears of happiness on all the Py's today. God, please bless my sister Marian and her family. Yes, we all wore pink for our sister today, even the brothers, there are no sissies in our Pie. I am saddened to say after over about 6 years of pain and suffering, and fighting the battle, at age sixty-three, our Mar has gone home to be with God, and Mom and Dad, (she left us the first day of September 2017). Our whole family was by her bedside to pray and send her with the angel home to Heaven. We will love, miss, and remember her always.

Richard Py, my 5th sibling, the hardest slice of the Pie.

I have been typing our stories with ease; however, this slice is a hard swallow. When my baby brother Richard was born on December 16, 1953 he was a healthy little baby. When he was about seven months old, he came down with the Chicken Pox. This was unusual, babies that young are supposed to be immune to these childhood diseases during the first nine months of their little life. Richard's case was very severe. He was covered from head to toe, including inside his mouth and ears with the poxes. It is a wonder to me, that our doctor did not have the baby admitted to the hospital. Mom did the best she could, rubbing a soothing lotion on him to help with the itch. The baby cried a lot, he was so young, and could not communicate what was bothering him. Eventually he recuperated back to a healthy baby and grew as a normal child. *So, we thought.* He was a mischievous little boy, as all boys are, the terrible two's etc. He started Incarnation school after kindergarten, at age seven because he was not six by the cutoff date of October 1st. While I was still living at home, it appears Richie was always being punished, and sent to his bedroom, for a timeout, or he would be lightly paddled for something or other. He had a very bad temper as a child. Rich would kick and scream in his room. These actions would annoy my father, and the punishment would be prolonged. Toward the end of second grade, the nuns at school deemed him incorrigible, and mom had to remove him from Incarnation School. She entered him in the public school, just across the street from Inky. It was the Marston School. My brother made it to the third grade in the public school, and not quite the end of that year; Richard was expelled from the school. Since I was married in 1963, and had my first child Jack, I was a stay at home mom. My poor mother was out working to help stay afloat with the never ending ongoing bills that accrued to keep the home going. Dad was in and out of work with the union at the time. Mother asked me if Richard could stay at my apartment until she could figure out how to deal with getting him schooled. Richie stayed with me for a while, at which time, I found out I was pregnant to have a second baby, and it would be too much for me to continue watching my nine-year-old brother. So, Richard went home. No truant-officer ever approached my mother and father regarding Richard not being in school? Mom begged the juvenile court system to help locate a special program, so he could attend a school. It took a while and finally a kind Judge placed him in St. Gabriel's Hall for wayward boys. I don't think he was wayward, but there was something wrong. St. Gabe's was in Phoenixville, PA. While Richard did better out there, as he had his own little dorm area, a desk to study at, a TV, and a one on one tutor, but he still had a tough time adjusting to this new atmosphere. In the late 50's and through the 60' a boy like Richard was just labeled a bad kid. So, until my brother was about twelve he had little or no schooling. While he was at St. Gabe's as they called it, he was being taught, but it was almost impossible for him to comprehend the studies that other children his age had become an expert in. While he was still at the Hall, when he was almost sixteen Richie, came down with pneumonia, and since St. Gabe's did not have a Doctor on staff. Richie was taken to Valley Forge Hospital to be treated. The Doctor in charge of my brother took a special interest in him and wanted to know why a boy as good as he was, while in the hospital, was placed in this institute for wayward boys. The good doctor ordered a series of test for Richie, and they determined he had something called, Minimal Brain Dysfunction. Today it is diagnosed and called Learning Deficit Disorder. Since Rich, could be treated with drugs as an outpatient, he no longer had to stay out in Phoenixville. While being treated on controlled doses of certain drugs, he could live a normal life. Normal for most people is not normal for all, especially for my brother. He would not be able to return to any school. They figured work would be better. The case worker would be looking into work for him to start earning an income. Now, the dilemma of how Richie was going to get back home. In early December, he was discharged, and mother asked if John and I would be kind enough to go to Phoenixville and bring him home. How could I say no to mom? That Saturday morning it started to snow early, by the time we reached St. Gabe's it was a blinding blizzard. My husband John T. was not a happy camper, because once on a Friday the thirteenth of September 1963, we offered to take my sister Pat to a Girl Scout Camp out in Skippack, PA. It was called, Laughing Waters. (Thinking back, John and I were not laughing). Mom also told me we must dump three black cats on any farm along the way. We did as requested, as I always did, but our car hit a railroad tie on a back r oad into the camp. The oil pan was ripped open, which we did not know until the automobile pistons ran dry of oil. That was the end our new but old car. Now here we were again doing Mom a favor and retrieving my brother, so he could be home for his birthday, on Dec 16th, for Christmas, and the rest of his life. We prayed all the way home for a safe trip while driving through the blinding blizzard. John T. Hopkins vowed, *"never again, do you hear me?"* *"Yes"* I replied, with crossed fingers. There were other trips; I am not caring to go into detail. We did do a lot of chauffeuring in our newer and bigger vehicles. Note, we had a few nine passenger Chevy Station Wagons over our years. Richard returned to society at age seventeen, he was able to find work in a few different bakeries and did an excellent job. He even met a girl named A... they married, and after about seven years of marriage they were blessed very quickly with two beautiful little girls. When Jenny the oldest, was a little more than a year or so, they had Vicky another baby. Things started going wrong in the marriage, and with my brother's meds, more and more, never enough and not prescribed correctly. A... his wife separated, then a divorce. Jenny was about twelve, her mom was no longer able to provide for her, and Richie was not doing well at all. My sister Jeannie and her husband Ed Merk took Jenny to live with them and their three sons, Eddie, Jeffrey, and Kenny. Vickie the younger child, at just about two years old, had already been living with my sister Pat and her husband George. Years have passed, and life for the girls has dealt them a better hand. Both are married to good men and Vickie has two wonderful sons. But my poor (and I do mean **poor**) brother Richard has been in and out (more out than in) homeless shelters. He was never a bad boy. The medical field back in the late 50' and 60's just labeled kids like him bad. He has done many things over the years that would make you think he is bad, no he was and still is sick. I think for one being in his mid-sixties, who could not get it together by now, he most likely never would. He is physically handicapped and must walk with a four-wheeled walker. He had been homeless up until Thursday May 21st, 2015 at which time my nice Karen Py Stewart called Habitat for Life, and they have placed him in living quarters. If you asked the family, this story could be told many ways. I think he has paid his dues. He was his own worst enemy. Let me quote a very small passage from one of the Acts of the Apostles, *"God has overlooked the times of ignorance"* I will overlook my brother's past mistakes. I am trying to understand, and now his part of our pie crust is a bit digestible. Richard at age 65 has turned his life around; he is a resident at Immaculate Heart of Mary Nursing Home at Holme Circle and the Roosevelt Blvd., Phila., PA. He is healed in heart, mind, and most of all his soul. God has forgiven and blessed my younger brother. So, has the family, they visit him, weekly, they probably don't realize it, but in doing so, they are practicing one of the corporal work of mercy; Visit the sick and impaired. Richie, God has forgiven you and so do I. NOTE: a bit of poetic justice, just recently Richie was moved to a new room. His new roommate was a Monsignor. Mother, I know, must have been beating poor God's ear off, as she did many times to the Catholic Priest she met during her life on earth. But as fast as it happened, God had other plans for the Monsignor. The Angels visited Richie's room and took the man of the holy cloth home to meet God and our mom. Richie will again have to adjust, he is doing a lot of good readjusting in the beginning of his golden years.

Kathleen my fourth sister

How does a beautiful name like Kathleen become Pete or Pizza Pie? Well the Pete I gave her. Kathleen takes after mom: she was the shortest of our siblings. When she was a baby, walking or should I say dancing? Pete was about two-foot-high; she didn't have much hair, and what she did have stood straight up in the air, almost like the crown on a rooster. At the time she looked more like a baby boy, than a girl, so with this description, I just gave her a nickname Pete. The name stuck with her into her sixties which she is now. Kathleen's looks have changed. Never portly, and a beautiful head of hair, like the rest of our family, she just sports that old nickname. Now Patty also calls her Pizza Py, I never asked why, but she answers to all three names. I never knew this about Kathleen, but when she started school a nun called mother to ask why the child does not answer to the name Kathleen, *"is that her name or what"*. Mom said, *"we all call her Pete"*, *"Well"* said the nun, *"you should start calling her by her birth given name"*. Mom couldn't even get Pete right, sometimes, when mother would be so worked up over who knows what, she would call Jeannie, Japetee, and Petey PaJeanie, we all still mimic mom from time to time, we would call the girls mom's mixed up names, just for old time sake.   Kathleen has two great loves, dancing, and animals. She, from the age of two, would hold out her arm, look at her thumb, and just spin around and around to the sound of any music. I got dizzy just watching her spin. She is our "Dancing Queen" like in that song. I call her our mover and groovier. Her next love was her pets, we had a dog named Scottie and a cat named Whiskers, and somewhere we acquired a hamster, Pete fell in love with the darn thing. It was always out of the cage. I kept thinking, one of these days, the whiskers on Whiskers may look a little moist? Mm! She would watch the hamster in the cage for hours. That animal also spun all day on its treadmill inside its cage. One day I came home and found the hamster's cage door open, and the thing was gone. I was sure the cat got it. Mom was always too busy to think about checking on the darn thing. I started looking all around for it. Now mom was helping and hoping to find it safe. I thought to myself, if one of us steps on it, it's a goner. Pete was almost four years old then. I looked around the house for her, thinking she was on one of here spinning trips. Nope, there she stood, with the hamster clamp in her tightly closed fist, she loved it to death, and need I say more. That's our Pete. Oh! Yes, there is one little scar I neglected to mention. Baby bottles were glass for the longest time. Pete could throw well for a baby. Mom asked me one evening if I would go and fetch Pete's empty bottle from her crib. Now things weren't always bright as they should be, Could it have been that our electric was temporarily shut off for some reason, I would guess lack of an on-time payment. Well I am crawling around the dark room trying to locate Pet's baby bottle, I never found the snap on nipple, but the palm of my right hand and a lot of red moisture coming from my palm, found the busted glass bottle. A trip to the hospital and five stiches in my right hand, I can still see the scar. I thank the maker of plastic baby bottles; no one will experience scarring.

My baby sister Jeannie

Someone must be last, I was first. Today May 30, **2015 the** last **will shine**. Regina Py Merk (Jean) she was born when I was a junior in Cardinal Dougherty High School. I was ashamed, not of the baby, but because my Mom was having a tenth child at age thirty-eight years old. I got over my embarrassment fast when I saw this beautiful baby girl. When she was two I took her everywhere, I was eighteen or nineteen and engaged to John T. Hopkins, people would ask *"What is your baby's name" "She is not my baby, she is my little sister"* I would reply, the people would say *"Oh, right"*? Just like when brother Joey had the long curly hair, and people would ask *what is your SISTERS name?* Questions I always answered the truth, no one would believe me. Since I married at age twenty and had four sons by the time I was twenty-four I cannot give you childhood stories about Jean.

When she was old enough to babysit or should I say kid sit, I would ask her to stay with the boys, when John and I would attempt to get a night out. My sister was just five years older than my first son Jack. Jean and Jack were closer in age, and they liked teasing Michael who was just four or

five years old at that time. Jean and Jack would play pranks on the younger children. This is a story I found out much after they pulled the stunt on Michael. When Ma (Bell Telephone) was the only phone company around, one could dial your own phone number, (GL5-6520) and it would ring in your home. Well Jean had Jack upstairs with my portable typewriter near the phone. Jean instructed Jack to dial our home number and start typing when she answered it down in the kitchen. As the phone rang, and Jean answered it, she had a one-way conversation, while Jack was typing away, she carried on her story. It went like this: *"Oh' yes this is the Hopkins house"*, *"yes"* she said into the dead phone, **Michael is adopted**". *His parents are out but give me your number and I will have them return the call, I am not sure if they are going to keep this boy."* Now in my kitchen stands this frightened little four to five-year-old boy listening to the pounding of the typewriter on the other end, thinking that the adoption agency was on the receiving end of the call. I again will certify, all four of my sons were born in four consecutive years. They were born in Holy Redeemer Hospital in Huntington Valley, Montgomery County, PA.

Sometime to this day Michael Francis Hopkins teases me about his doubts, as to whether he was adopted. I did not find out about this caper for a long time. I do not think I used Jean to stay with the boys after I found out that my fourth son was adopted. It was news to me and Mike's dad. I started to used neighborhood girls to stay with the boys, but my sons were getting older and did not want a girl sitter. Enter Ed Merk

I met Ed Merk on the air, while operating our citizen-band radio. I would hear a lady come on about ten at night, she had a shy voice, she would say, "Breaker, this is Whistler's Mother, *has anyone seen, or heard him on the radio? If so, tell him to get home, he has school tomorrow"*, or *"it is past curfew."* A CB, (Citizen Band Radio) break was due one Saturday and I was quite curious to see this Whistler person. John T. and I met him in person, while attending the coffee break, he was just turning fourteen, and we thought he would be a good sitter for our four sons. Whistler was his radio band name. Ed was also the youngest of four sons. I did not know it at the time, but as years passed, and Ed kept coming to our home. long after the boys did not need a sitter, and he was in the US

Army, I began to wonder, does this young man have a crush on me, I think he did. I never did learn my lesson about curiosity. I had to send him packing, or at least set him in a better direction. On Christmas night, 1975 he was at our home, and he was annoying one of John T. Hopkins **old maid** aunts, (Agnes), with his exaggerated tales. So, I asked him, "Ed, *would you like to meet my baby sister Jeannie?*" *"You have a sister?" I liked this, a question to a question. "Wow yes call her I will take her out."* Finally! I thought I would get rid of Ed. Never in my wildest dreams did I think he would end up my brother in law, and a good husband to Jean and a dad to my three nephews. Jean and Ed married young, and they had three sons, Eddie, Jeffrey, and Kenny. I am sad to say Ed died in his forties, fifteen years ago in February 2003. It was the winter, but he was only in the spring of his life. Like me, my sister Jeanie found Ed dead when she returned home from work. I am glad I sent him packing to a little piece of the Py. Jean and Ed took on the responsibility of helping raise Jenny Py when she was just twelve years old; she was the oldest one of my brother Richards two daughters. Jean and Ed were as poor as we Py's were, when they were struggling as a younger married couple, but would not let a Py girl go without a home. Jean works in Adams Town, PA at Baumann Hat Co. She is on her feet most of the day, and her poor hands hurt from bending straw in the hat production. I wish she did not have to work, it is sort of like, Rapunzel with the golden hair, she too had to spin straw into gold, in the end Rapunzel was rewarded. Jeanie my dear sister you will be rewarded a hundred times for your thoughtfulness and generous heart. You made a statement back in April 2015, you said, "*When I was down and out, all of you helped me, now I am able to help my sister Marian*" **In my eyes you are not last, but first**. *Hoping that the fundraiser you started for our sister Marian's cancer cost is a considerable success today like you are. Good Luck, I love you; your Big Sis, Elaine.*

Enough tears next is a laugh.

The Playtex Girdle's (Mom's)

No one will believe it. It was worth its elastic in gold. Let me try to explain.

As I said in the beginning, mom was a very petite person. Really no need for a girdle, but women wore them to give them a better posture, and a tighter body. Mom wore her garment to the last day. It was always a Playtex, and it was the open-end kind with the garter straps attached, to hold up her sometimes-runny seamed stockings. Years have gone by since that was the style. Mom used her girdle for other purposes. Mother kept her money in her elastic garment while wearing it, not that we children, or dad would take her dough; she just thought it was safe, and snug there. She was sure no one would ever grab her purse and get her money. I guess she was right in a way, about the cash part, but the pocketbook was another problem. For as long as I can remember, Mom was always looking for her pocketbook. Oh! After a big fuss, and a lot of running up, and down, in and out, someone, or Mom would locate the bag, and we could get heading wherever we were going. Her whole life was in that purse.

Now *mothers girdle* gave up a lot of secrets, and surprises. She would get a new one for several reasons. First, if it was not tight enough to keep the cash nice, tight, and safe. As tight as she had to be with a dollar her cash was safe. Of course, there would be the need to acquire a new one for a special occasion, like a wedding, or a baptism, or even if she was invited to attend a surprise shower for someone. Could it be my wedding shower? Yes, it was. I would have been totally surprised at both of my wedding showers, if it had not been for mom's undergarment. She always had to wait until payday to purchase the darn (I mean elastic) thing. Payday was always a Friday, and on the Saturday before any of the above events, mother would state she was on her way to get a new girdle. **This was one of the only things she ever told us about personal stuff,** which we did not have to know, but for some reason or another she would advise all of us of her upcoming new purchase.

A month or so prior to our marriage, John T. Hopkins, and I, were heading back to grandmom' s at the 27th street address, and I could not for the life of me, figure out why John was taking me there that night. He said it would be nice to just visit with my grandmom before we got married, but halfway there, it dawned on me, *oh; mom got a new girdle this past Saturday.* I put it together; the wedding shower was at grandmom' s house. We got there about 7:00 PM on a week night; I opened the door like I owned the place. To my surprise, I was not surprised. Can you imagine my disappointment? no one was in the living room, or dining room. My Uncle John was sitting on the sofa reading the evening Bulletin. I then got the brainy idea, it was in the basement. I quick ran to the cellar door and turned on the light. No one was there. My fiancée asked, "*What are you looking for*". I made up a story; I wanted to see my grandmother. Well, as your uncle stated, "*She went out*". My grandmother never went out alone. But being that two of her daughters, my Aunts Peggy and Helen lived not far from her, they may have had her with them. Well a trip for nothing, I thought. I asked John, to walk up to Dick Crain's department store so we could get some things for our up and coming new apartment. "*Ok" we can do that.* We got two large lamp shades, and then John said, "*Why don't we stop around the corner to Marston Street and see your Aunt Helen before we get the R bus home. OK, I loved going to her home.* We walked up her steps, rang the bell, and she yelled, "*Come right in",* how strange was that, I thought. Don't they keep their door locked? Well, I threw open the door, and lights keep flashing in my eyes, and people calling out *surprise*. There it was my wedding shower. I knew the new girdle was purchased to be worn to my shower, I thought I was too smart, that it was at grandma's house. Well they outsmarted me, because, mom had mentioned her girdle slipping and stated she shopped for the new garment and thought I would have caught on that the shower was soon. I had the night correct, but they changed the place, just to make sure I got surprised. I sure did. So, Mom's girdle told it all.

In the beginning, I told you of my husband HOPPY, John T. Hopkins, the unreachable guy for me. Well he was to be mine to have and to hold in sickness, and in health, for richer or poorer, until death do us part. We, the two of us started our life together on Saturday, January 5, 1963. We danced at our wedding to Moon River, the theme song in the movie, Breakfast at Tiffany's. We went to the theater to see this new Box Office hit film. While sitting in the dark, watching, and listening to the movie, we thought it would be the perfect song to dance to at the wedding. John T., and I were off to see the world, and we did not know what was ahead for us. We laughed together, when we said we would *never be able to have breakfast at Tiffany's, let alone, make a purchase at that upscale jewelry store located in NY City.* That part of the movie, to us, was never a dream. But living our life together until death do us part was a reality. Our life together, in the beginning was a work of art. We were poor of cash, but rich in love. Yes, we had our ups, and downs. Everyone has problems between each other, this is life. But in this life of ours, we brought four healthy, handsome sons into the world, in just about four years of each other. I was beginning to think, I would be like mom, always wearing that maternity type wardrobe, but not a girdle. We had to watch out, if we had one more baby, and it turned out to be a girl, we would not have room for all to have a comfortable bed, or bedroom to rest their little heads on. So, we decided to stop while we were ahead.

John Kennedy Hopkins (Jack) named after JFK was our first boy. He is now fifty-four years old. He is a detective in the Philadelphia Police Department. In case anyone does not know this; Jack was the youngest police officer ever appointed to the detective department in the city of Phila., and I think he still may hold the record? He is married to Linda Plummer, and they have three loving adult children, Jessie Lee, Laura Anne, Katie, and six grandchildren and one great grand baby. They are, (Dominick Jr)., Jessie Lee, Jr. Nicholas D. Seraphina Hopkins, (Lucas Gavin, and Liam Been) Katie is not married yet. Jack & Linda are proud of G Grand Dominick Jr. 3/2018. Jack will be a volunteer Firemen 5/14/18. Feasterville Fire Co.

Kevin Joseph, number two son age fifty-three, named Kevin because I knew he would be, a Kevin from Heaven when he grew up. Joseph was in honor of his grandfather Joseph Hopkins. I never met Mr. Joseph Hopkins, he died at age sixty-three when my husband John T. Hopkins was only fifteen years old, John T. lost his dad and best friend the night he found his father dying in his bedroom, just after Mr. Hopkins returned home from work. My Kevin is a Philadelphia Firefighter; his father John would be elated. Kevin married Jacquelyn A. Yanussie; they have four adult children, Jessica Lynn, Brittney Anne, Jacklyn Elizabeth, and Kevin Patrick, who was born on St. Patrick's Day 1991. They are blessed with The Little Man, Noah Cole O'Brien, Jessica, and Dave's son. Kevin is involved in his church and was in Boy Scouting for many years. He is always there to help with people in need.

Stephen William, my third boy, and my "la de da boy, a little song I made up to sing to all my sons when they were babies", Stephen always wanted me to sit with him and sing that silly song to him. He is named Stephen because it is a saint's name, and a strong one. (the first martyr) The William is after my dad. Steve as we call him is a self-made man, married to Peggy Ann Minerly, and they have three adult children, Patrick Francis, former Cpl. USMC., Jenna Minerly Hopkins, a Gwyneth Mercy Grad, she is to marry Matt M in July 2018 and Stephen J. USAF, Senior Airman, married to Danielle. Steve and Peggy are grandparents to Pat's daughter Shallie B. who lives on the West Coast in CA, with her parents.

Peg and Steve are waiting for their East Coast grand baby from Stephen (Bucky) and his wife Danielle soon., it will be a boy. Stephen W. is a 34-year Acme employee and Peggy and Steve own a Tasty Kake route. They are gearing toward a young retirement, already setting goals with a Condo at the Jersey shore. They look forward to a condo in FL. They will have a winter- summer hook up.

Michael Francis, our fourth son, who I thought at his birth, God would bless me with a girl, I had picked the name Michelle out for the new baby, but when the doctor announced a bouncing baby boy, I had to think fast, so I bounced back quickly with the name Michael Francis, and for the record, (**he is my birth given son**. "Not adopted, Mike" and to my kid sister, your aunt Jeannie.) Mike is making himself and his wife into young entrepreneurs, as they are running many Fed-X Ground delivery truck. routes. He is married to Nicole Refino and has two young children. Michael Peter, nine years old, and Izabella Nicole eight years young. Since they had their children much later than Mike's brothers, I now, at age seventy-five am trying to be a good grandmom to the latest of my loving grandchildren. John T. Hopkins would have loved them in his old age, as he did our other ten grandchildren.

HOPPY the HUBBY

I would like to tell you all about that exciting and surprising life John T. and I lived, but all that is really a start of another book. I do want to tell one exciting, and surprise that happened to me in my tenure as a wife to John T. No one ever knew what to expect with John in their life. He was a very good provider, we were not rich, or at least I thought we weren't. He was a self-taught electrician, no technical school for him, at twelve; he would follow the Philadelphia Electric high wire trucks around. The crew all knew this curious kid, so the men on their lunch breaks would show him the tools, and explain various aspects of wiring, and connections to him. He was Mr. Electric. John read books on how to and he did it. With that behind him, while working a full-time job as *head electrician and maintenance for the Philadelphia Parking Authority*, he would moonlight (*I like that*) moon light, it always reminds me of our dancing days. While he did work on the side for all our married life and was paid well. He never used his extra monies for part of our income, and never put it in the bank. I never got a good reason from him as why he would hide the cash that he paid taxes on at the end of each year, proof with his 1099s. Well I guess I should say to each his own. But John would put his rainy-day cash in envelopes; he would date and total each one of them and hide the money in the drop ceilings in our home. Late one night while he was sleeping, and I watching the Johnny Carson show, as I relaxed on the sofa, I heard this plop coming from the drop ceiling. Thinking it sounded like some sort of animal, more like a squirrel, from the loud thump, it dawns on me about John wealth up above my head. O no! I thought to myself, as John was up in bed snoring, we must have a mouse. No, I just heard another one, now it is mice, and they make their nest out of paper. You and I both know they are blind, so they would not be choosy as to different type of paper, money or not, to begin a nice winter nest. If you think Santa, flew up the chimney fast, I beat him by minutes up the steps to our bed room, to jolt the snoring master of the house. I mentioned his stash of cash, and the mice running around in his so-called bank, as he was taking a nice awaking stretch. When what I was telling him settled in his fogged head, he flew out of bed faster than I ran up the steps. In no time the money was removed from the ceilings. He took the envelopes out from the living room ceiling, and put it all, I thought, in a locked steel cash box, but that was only part of his wealth, he had been hoarding money for so long, he forgot half of the cash, thank the Lord, the mice forgot it too. After John died, Stephan found at least four yellowed envelopes full of old bills lying in a corner of the bedroom ceiling. I had called Steve about an electrical problem in a light in that room, that is when he told me he saw envelopes up there, "no *Steve, I said, "Dad removed all his money when we had the mice.*" Steve said to me "well if that is the case, I will just take these envelopes out of up here and keep them." When all was done, between the cash I got from the lockbox in the bedroom, the night John died, and now the newly found envelops full of old cash. I thought we were just getting by, in those lean and hungry years, when the children were very young. I ended up with many thousands of dollars. When I needed a fresh loaf of bread, and just made toast with the old bread, to save a dollar I think I could hang him, but he was already gone. He had all that "bread" stuffed away, and I pinched pennies for the longest time. There are many Hopkins stories, maybe a whole book of them, but this is a Py story.

In keeping with "A Slice of the PIE", I will try to bring my Py story to an end, but not before I state, I never thought I would miss my first John's antics and all his quirks. John was loved by all, never an enemy, and his son's loved, and learned a lot from him. Electric was his forte, and he certainly electrified me from the first day I saw him, when I was just a high school girl. Please John, husband of mine, rest in peace, I will see your smile, and that penguin walk of yours again someday, just as I saw you walking away from our car, after I gave you the last kiss goodbye, the morning I dropped you at the Einstein Hospital for a routine test, on the last day of your life. If only I knew, I would have never left you alone that morning, or alone the night you died, without anyone by your side. I found John at the front door, with the dog's leash in his hand, he was on one knee leaning against a chair, the dog and the two cats were sitting watch for me. Please, all forgive me. No one should die alone. John T. lived a life that was full, loving me, and our four sons. He enjoyed his job as Chief Electrician, and Maintenance man for the PPA (Philadelphia Parking Authority). John also belonged to the Philadelphia Second Alarmers Association; it was his passion to help the fire department. John T. Hopkins and I never got off to see the world. We traveled very little, he loved Philadelphia, and never wanted to go too far from home and the city he loved, but he took me through the world with him, as we traveled it, in all the books he read. He loved to read about history and geography. We traveled the world through his National Geographic magazines. Every dream he had was lived through his broad reading of history and geography magazines John, our dreams, little or big will always be a part of me. I can't believe I was not with you when you left this earth without me, for HOME. Your last words on the phone to me at 7:10 PM, November 30, 1999, were "I'll see you when you get home." I am not HOME YET. Old Blue eyes would sing a song, with these words in it, "And now the end is near, so I face the final curtain". I do hope it came down fast, and, you did not suffer.

A quote of Love. Love Inspired, "And now these three remain: faith, hope, and love. But the greatest of these is Love." 1 Corinthians 13:13

I copy to you, an in-memory poem, of an unknown author

"If I had seen you to the last and held your dying hand; and heard the last sigh from your heart I would not feel so bad. I did not know the pain you had; I did not see you die. I only know you went far away and never said good-by."

"That we once enjoyed, and deeply loved, we can never lose, for all that we love deeply becomes part of us." **This is a quote from Helen Keller.**

John, I just wanted to tell you from my heart what was always on my mind, I hope you can hear me?

As I wrote, and, read his eulogy, in St. Helena Church after John's funeral Mass, it may be repetitive to parts in this story. I was the only one that could do John's eulogy at his funeral. I knew him best. It went like this:

This is to my loving husband, a father, brother, grandfather, uncle, and friend. *He was first known to me as, Johnny, Jack, and Hoppy. "John Thomas Hopkins", when he made me angry.*

How do I begin? When the end has just come? In 1958 the early part of my junior year of high school, I first saw this tall handsome, older than I guy, at a viewing (can you imagine that) "a viewing", where here on December 7, 1999, I will now see this still tall handsome, tattered older man for the last time on earth; that is. ("A Day that will live in Infamy".) John was everywhere I went for the next two years. I did not know where he came from, or who he was, but to my young youthful eyes, he was someone important, at the time, I had no clue how significant he would become to me. I saw him at a young Democrat rally for JFK for President, then I knew he was somebody meaningful and, too far from my reach. "Me"? One of the ten Py kids from 2nd Street; I did not think we could ever get together. Well as time flew by and in Jan 1961, I found myself at the Boulevard Pools Ballroom dance, and by chance I was introduced to no other than the man of the hour, "John". Cupid was a little slow getting started, it took till mid-February for "Dapper Dan" to ask me out; we never parted until, Tuesday November 30, 1999 when I entered my home, to find John's lifeless body on the floor. You know, after getting to know John, I found we were predestined to our death. Both being born in Roxborough Memorial Hospital, baptized in St. Bridget's church, and of course married in the same church Incarnation of Our Lord, and still unbeknown to us at the time, our parent's grave sites were four rows away from each other in the same lot area at the same cemetery, where John is to be laid for a long overdue rest.

I must say we had our trials, and tribulations, and our ups, and downs over our almost thirty-seven years of happily, and sometimes not so happy married bliss. My sons will agree with me, John was a loving husband, best father, a civic minded and giving man. He was my **encyclopedia,** our Mr. Fixit, one of the best weathermen, better than Wally Kinnan, the weather man and ACCU weather at times. John was the true love of my life. I will miss him and all his "Noise" so very much. The walls of our home are now **SILENT**, and if I could have just one wish, it would be to hear

*John yelling, "Elaine listen to this, or watch that on TV, but wishes like this one, are impossible, and I will have to continue to have a **"Silent Night"**, which was one of my John's favorite Christmas hymns. So, my **LOVE** good bye, and be very quiet up in heaven, it is supposed to be a peaceful place. Yes John, I am still telling you what to do. Heaven will never ever, be the same again. The Lord has met John T. Hopkins!*

Love till I meet you at the pearly gates, when I am finely home with you, and Our Lord. Elaine

I had a flashback; It was a Friday evening, Aug. c2014 My husband, John C. Lynch and I attended a concert performed by the Cardinal Dougherty Alumni Band, the only thing alive from our wonderful school. Well as, the band played, Moonlight Serenade, one of the songs, my first John T. and I dance to while preparing for our life together. At that moment, as the band leader said, "Instruments up" and the melody began, I closed my eyes, and we John T, you, and I, were dancing at the Brookline *Ballroom, we were gliding across the dance floor. The room was dark; the silver ball reflecting from the ceiling would shoot a glimmer of spot light on us. I was back* *with you, in your arms for a few moments in time. You know, "we were off to see the world", like the two in the song, **"Moon River".*** Then the music stopped, and I was returned to the picnic bench as dusk began to settle upon the concert. *I sat with my now husband of almost 15 years, John C. Lynch, your old friend from the CD band fathers; we continued listening to some of the Glen Miller music of our era, 1960's and earlier. You John T. were there in spirit with us, it was a wonderful evening.*

No Final Steps Yet

*I am old in years, but not in my mind, and heart. I think I shall be around for a few more good years. I would like to see this story in lights, but that is also **wishful thinking**, I have done my share of that in the last seventy-five years. I hope this story will be an enjoyment, and something of an" incitement" a meaningful contribution to all my family members and readers. It will most likely be put on a book shelf in one's library, or kept, **as a** reference about the PY heritage, and this is my purpose for the story. I did what my Father wanted to do. I am still here and doing well, but when I am gone, and none of us know how we will be when our* *life comes to an end, do know this; **all must go**, look at our family tree, and remember me.*

I am adding another poem by an unknown author to the ending; it caught my eye, and then my heart, it was on the program at a funeral of a much older lady than I. It was written for a <u>Mom</u>. I tried to locate the author but failed, so a credit is due to the author?

A limb has fallen from the family tree

I keep hearing a voice that says, "Grieve not for me.

Remember the best times, the laughter, and the song.

The good life I lived while I was strong.

Continue my heritage, I am counting on you.

Keep smiling, and surely the sun will shine through.

Rest in Peace Mom

My mind is at ease, my soul is at rest.

Remembering all how I truly was blessed Continue traditions, no matter how small.

Go on with your life, do not worry about falls.

I miss you all dearly, so keep up your chin.

Until the day comes we are together again.

Meaningful poems like this remind me of our Marian, whose life was cut short by Cancer, in the September of her years, on the first day of September 2017. I penned this on the eve of what would have been her 64th BD.

Stepping-Down

*To, my family, friends, and readers this is the final piece of, "A Slice of the Pie "I hope you enjoyed reading it, as much as I enjoyed reminiscing back to a time, when the world was so different, when a child could play outside, without a parent worrying. When you could leave you front door open, your car unlocked, **if you had one**, and if you forgot, (Mom) and left your handbag outside, it would still be there. See Mom, you never had to put your cash in your girdle back in the olden days. Life was simpler and so very different then now, c.2017-18. Any young children, or young adults, reading this story **now**, just think? The c.2015-2030 or so will be **you're olden days**. You will not be able to reminisce like I did,* to a time like that one, *when you are in* *your seventies, because our wonderful world has, and will continue to change. So, as I step down, in the last chapter of my public life, and quietly enjoy the rest of my golden years I suggest that you try to remember, **"From dust thou art, and to dust you will return", it is in the Bible. Remember God, <u>He will remember you</u>. Stay close to Him, Death comes like a Thief in the Night, and you may not have the chance, or be able to say, "I am sorry Lord; forgive me, because I forgot you God". I want to see all my family, friends, and foe in Heaven when all ends, This too shall come to pass. (The world on earth).***

When I am gone, remember, I enjoyed every minute of my life; I laughed a lot and told my PY stories that made you all laugh. Please all of you have a drink on me, make mine Amaretto, Da Vinci will due on ice, my favorite. Disaronno is too expensive for the Irish wake. I will have one tonight.,

Love from me to all.

Elaine B. Py (Hopkins) Lynch

About the Author

A wife twice, Hopkins-Lynch, mother, grandmother, a total of four sons, twelve grandchildren, five great grandchildren she laughed, as she comments about stuffing cash in envelopes for all, on special occasions like her mom did. She was born, raised, and attended parochial schools in Philadelphia, PA. She's the oldest child of parents who raised ten children; the family in this book. She calls herself a working girl. Customer Service is her forte.

First job working at a 5 & 10 cent store, at the age of fifteen, just a clerk.

While in high school c.1959, she sought out a position in an Insurance Office, she remained working there until her first child would be born.

She left the work force for nine years, c1964 to 1973, to be a stay at home mom and raise her four sons that came four years in a row. (Happy Days)

Returning to work in 1973 selling Drugs, (legally) in Telemarking- called, (A CALL GIRL selling drugs), get that, she laughs about the title.

Broadening her capabilities, she left the drug world, and worked for a company who supplied protective gear to Nuclear Plants. From a 5 & 10 cent store, to a nuclear world, she just kept changing her hat. How about the home of the DOT, it's all about the printed matter, she entered a world with new nomenclature, where plates were not what you eat from, and blankets did not keep you warm, rollers were not for your hair, and burning a plate without a fire meant something entirely different. All this, and more, she began selling for the Printing Industry, starting out with Polychrome Corp. known in the Printing industry as "The Home of the Dot", she did not know about the dot or printing, but secured the position anyway.

After the company moved all the sales girls to Tarry town, NY, across the river from the home office in Yonkers. She took a leave from work to be a stay at home mom again to her 4 teen age sons. In September of 1982 with her sons back to school, she was sought out by Franklin Printing Supply Co. to spearhead a customer service department. She stayed in the printing industry for fourteen years. Next, she ventured into the American Flag business for Humphry's Flag Co. in old city, PA, near Betsy Ross House. After working in the flag design world, she went to school, not to teach, but as a teacher's aide in the public schools in Phila., and she sold tires for the Firestone Tire Co. Next was in the Silk Screen World, all about embroidery, and printing on tees, hats, and golf shirts. Not being satisfied she entered the Mortgage World, working for a subprime lending company Thinking she was not done work yet, she ventured into the DNA world of molecular testing as a Customer Service Rep. for Lab Repco. After she re-met, and married, John C. Lynch, the boy in the brown suit, from high school, he said, "**Enough work for you**". She left the work force on June 3, 2003. Not enough to keep her busy, she decided to write a book, the one her father wanted to do, but God had other plans for

Bill Py. This story is her version of what she thought might have been what her Father wanted to do. After thirty-five years, out in the working world, never without a job. She started typing for herself, and her payment came in the form of contentment, to be able to relive her life with her family as a PY (PIE) girl. She uses an old proverb she once read; "Growing Old Beats the Alternative of Dying Young" How true in her father's story that did not come to life.

From the Author of, A Slice of the Pie

Elaine Py Hopkins Lynch

In developing topics for my story, first was the reason I wrote this book. My father Bill Py had a wish to write a story about his life as a Py and his youth. Dad's life was cut short on his fifty-sixth birthday, God had other plans for dad. A Slice of the Pie was supposed to be his story, but in writing it, the book had to be about my life as a Py rather of dad's.

The Py's history goes as far back to the 16th Century, I was told by dad's half-brother Bobby Py. The Py's lived and were involved in Knighthood in the early part of that century. I begin my story with our history dating from 1760 into 2018 in this 21st century. I tell of the beginning of my timeline 1942 to present day, I also include my grandparents paternal and maternal ancestry. I emphasize about the two moves from the first home I began my life in.

Looking back through past years, my feelings were not a result of any of my actions but caused by circumstance that evolved during the early years of my parent's lives that occurred beyond their control. In a book I read, before starting this true story, "How to Write My Memoirs, or a Book". It asked many questions of the author. The question I though most important was; **Thinking back, could you (me) have altered what happened in the early 1940's-50s, in my life.** After contemplating long and hard, with a clear mind, my answer was, **"Absolutely not".** It was not until the mid to very late 1950's that I was capable to recognize and change situations that affected my future life. As you have read, my chance to change my path in life occurred. I know God placed my seed of life in the Py family for many reasons; I would not have fit in anywhere else. I grew, learned, loved, and was loved unconditionally in my life as a Py girl on Second Street in Philadelphia, Pa. It made me a strong and better person. A word to the wise, **"Never wish you** were someone else, or born into a different family. I loved my life and my family.

See a photos on pg. 267, of the 10 Py siblings in 2017, and dad in his US Army Uniform c.1941. We are all in this photo. Our names are, Elaine, Billy, Patty, Marie, Joey, Richie, Marian, Kathleen-Pete, Denny, and Jeannie. Try to ID us.

No not another "HAT", no just my Easter Bonnet. Myakka River, Pt. Charlotte, FL in the background. Easter April 1, 2018.

Remembering:

The members of Rowland Community Center Seniors, who helped with the dedication part back in 2012.

To the Board of Directors of the League of the Sacred Heart of Jesus, for Police, Fire and Public Safety and all its members in Phila., PA of which I am a trustee. The Phila. Second Alarmers. American Legion Ladies AUX, Unit-100, Wyndmoor, PA., and Marine Corps League Ladies AUX Unit 281 which I am a member of both. Not to mention the volunteer cleaners of my church, Presentation BVM, Cheltenham, PA.

The Girl Scouts, Cub and Boy Scouts of America.

A big thanks to Robert M. Tokarek MD, he saved my skin. 4/18/18 Abington Derma.

To my friend Ethel, from Lucy, as we called ourselves, while clowning around, at the Enterprise Car Rental. Jane you know who you are, we laugh.

The art drawling is by Patrick McElroy a grandson of Joe and Pat Farley

In telling on dad, this Thanksgiving eve story, was the one, that people would say, **"You ought to write a book."** While, Joe read out loud and got such a kick about the live turkey, his grandson Patrick, a first-year college student, did a free hand drawing. A comic of, Mom giving dad "what for," as dad wonders why? He told her, **"I got the bird."** Yes a live one? Dad can do no wrong. One of my brothers said, "Can we keep it?" as mom shouted, "No we will eat it." Boo! As you have read, my sibling's boycotted the turkey part of that dinner, thank heavens for Hot Dogs

None of us Py's had any problem eating this bird, when cooked. Oh; and yes, we always stuffed the bird the night before Thanksgiving, so it would be ready, to be put in the oven early on Thursday, Thanksgiving Day. No one in our family had ever gotten sick from stuffing the bird the night before. eh

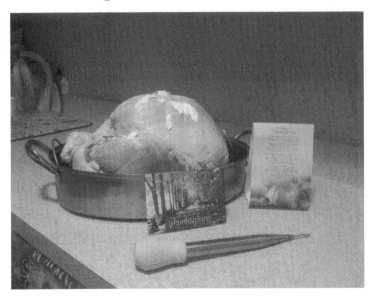

For Notes: *